The Forensic Documentation Sourcebook

The Forensic Documentation Sourcebook

A Comprehensive Collection of Forms and Records for Forensic Mental Health Practice

Theodore H. Blau, Ph.D.

John Wiley & Sons, Inc.

New York • Chichester • Weinheim • Brisbane • Singapore • Toronto

---

Note about Photocopy Rights

The Publisher grants purchasers permission to reproduce handouts from this book for their own professional use.

Library of Congress Cataloging-in-Publication Data:

Blau, Theodore H.
    The forensic documentation sourcebook : a comprehensive collection
of forms and records for forensic mental health practice / by
Theodore H. Blau.
        p.   cm.
    Includes bibliographical references.
    ISBN 0-471-25459-2 (pbk./disk : alk. paper)
    1. Forensic psychiatry—United States—Forms. 2. Forensic
psychiatry. I. Title.
KF8965.A65B58   1999
614′.1—dc21   98-16154

Printed in the United States of America.

10 9 8 7 6 5 4 3 2 1

Practice Planner Series Preface

The practice of psychotherapy has a dimension that did not exist 30, 20, or even 15 years ago—accountability. Treatment programs, public agencies, clinics, and even group and solo practitioners must now justify the treatment of patients to outside review entities that control the payment of fees. This development has resulted in an explosion of paperwork.

Clinicians must now document what has been done in treatment, what is planned for the future, and what the anticipated outcomes of the interventions are. The books and software in this Practice Planner series are designed to help practitioners fulfill these documentation requirements efficiently and professionally.

The Practice Planner series is growing rapidly. It now includes not only the original *Complete Psychotherapy Treatment Planner* and the *Child and Adolescent Psychotherapy Treatment Planner,* but also *Treatment Planners* targeted to specialty areas of practice, including: chemical dependency, the continuum of care, couples therapy, older adult treatment, employee assistance, pastoral counseling, and more.

In addition to the *Treatment Planners,* the series also includes *TheraScribe®: The Computerized Assistant to Psychotherapy Treatment Planning* and *TheraBiller™: The Computerized Mental Health Office Manager,* as well as adjunctive books, such as the *Brief Therapy, Chemical Dependence, Couples,* and *Child Homework Planners, The Psychotherapy Documentation Primer,* and *Clinical, Forensic, Child, Couples and Family,* and *Chemical Dependence Documentation Sourcebooks*—containing forms and resources to aid in mental health practice management. The goal of the series is to provide practitioners with the resources they need in order to provide high-quality care in the era of accountability—or, to put it simply, we seek to help you spend more time on patients and less on paperwork.

ARTHUR E. JONGSMA, JR.
Grand Rapids, Michigan
Series Editor

Contents

Contents

Contents

Contents

Contents

Contents

Disk Contents

Disk Contents

Disk Contents

Introduction

All professional psychological work should be accurate and ethical. Errors of omission or commission are likely to have the most serious repercussions in forensic psychological practice. In this setting, even small mistakes can lead to embarrassment, criticism, licensing board sanctions, and possible criminal charges as well as civil lawsuits. The devil is in the details.

The Forensic Documentation Sourcebook provides the structures likely to improve quality of forensic psychological practice, enhance the reputation and credibility of the forensic psychologist, and prevent improper or unfortunate occurrences.

Almost all of the forensic psychologist's work is within the framework of adversary judicial activity. Opposing counsels will search for errors or omissions that might suggest incompetence or questionable credibility. The forensic psychologist should view this reality as a challenge and an opportunity to demonstrate professional competence. The forms and procedural outlines herein were designed to help accomplish this goal. (For process details see Blau, T. (1998). *The Psychologist as Expert Witness,* 2nd ed. New York: John Wiley & Sons.)

The Forensic Documentation Sourcebook

Chapter 1

Initiating Forms

FORM 1
Forensic Intake

The Forensic Intake Form is the tool for initiating a forensic consultation. Usually filled out by the forensic psychologist, it is best done in one or two interviews with the retaining attorney (or rarely with a referring judge or his or her assistant or clerk when the psychologist is court-appointed). Some of the information will emerge from the attorney's description of the case while some areas will require the psychologist to ask questions. Form 1a is a completed Forensic Intake Form in a personal injury case where the retaining attorney represents a defendant in a civil matter.

Abbreviations

Dr—The hourly fee for the forensic psychologist.

Ret—The retainer (against which fees will be charged).

Res—Library or research work by assistants.

Tr—Test room charges (using a psychometrist).

FORM 2
Charge Sheet

The charge sheet should be started as soon as the retaining attorney agrees to the forensic psychologist's terms of engagement. This usually occurs during the Forensic Intake interview (Form 1a). A charge should be made for time spent on the case by the psychologist or staff. A copy of the charge sheet should be enclosed with the monthly invoice for services sent to the retaining attorney.

FORM 3
Terms of Agreement Letter

FORM 4
Terms of Engagement Contract

This letter (Form 3), prepared on the forensic psychologist's letterhead with the terms of engagement entered in the appropriate spaces should be sent to the retaining attorney, together with Form 4. When Form 3 is returned to the psychologist, signed by the retaining attorney, the contract for services is made. As a courtesy, two copies of Form 3 should be sent.

FORM 5
Case Chronology

During the deposition or at trial, the expert witness is likely to be asked by opposing counsel to state when the intake call was made, when various materials were received, when testing or interviews took place, or other events easily forgotten in a complex case. The purpose may be to confuse the witness or to suggest that the psychologist's memory is faulty. All this can be short-circuited by having the Case Chronology Form annotated as the case proceeds and making the form a part of the case file, readily available when needed.

FORM 6
Case Material Received

For purposes similar to that served by Form 5, this form is used to create a time log of all materials received that the psychologist might be using as part of the expert role.

FORM 7
Case Materials Sent

During the course of a forensic case, the psychologist may forward a variety of things to various parties. Again, the psychologist may be called upon to recall what was sent, when and to whom.

FORM 8
Forensic Intake Sheet
(Pre-Examination)

The Forensic Intake sheet provides basic data concerning the plaintiff or defendant who is to be interviewed and/or examined by the psychologist who has been retained to be an expert witness. This sheet should be completed prior to the first meeting except for appointments that are scheduled later in the evaluation process.

Some of the information can be obtained from the office of the retaining attorney. The remaining information can be obtained from the subject by telephone at the time the first appointment is scheduled.

FORM 9
Preselection Interview Form

More and more forensic psychologists are providing selection services to various public safety agencies (police, fire, emergency medical service, and so forth) at the local, state, and federal levels.

Preselection testing batteries have been developed and validated [see Blau, T. (1994). *Psychological Services for Law Enforcement*. New York: John Wiley & Sons].

Preliminary to conducting such an assessment, it is usual to conduct an interview with the candidate.

Form 1   Forensic Intake

Date:

Attorney:

Telephone:

Firm: Office:

Address: Home:

Fax:

E-Mail:

Case Style:

- [ ] Plaintiff (Pros., Pet.)
- [ ] Defendant
- [ ] Amicus Curia

Facts:

- [ ] Court Appointed

To Do   Schedule

Hypothetical Questions: Fees: Ret: $

Dr:

Tr:

Res:

- [ ] Discuss Fee Structure
- [ ] Request Initial Letter
  - Designate as consultant
  - Fees pd. on 30-day basis
  - Will send agreement letter
- [ ] Suggest Retrieval of Records and Information
- [ ] Discuss Pretrial Meeting

Anticipated Trial Date:

Judge:

- [ ] Confirming Letter Received

Court:

- [ ] First Appointment Scheduled

Asst/Secy to Attorney:

- [ ] CV Sent

Additional:

Form 1a   Forensic Intake

Date: *2/1/98*

Attorney: *John N. Surridge, Esq.*

Telephone:

    Office: *(813) 257-6349*

Firm: *Batton, Davis and Shakelton*

    Home: *Prefers not to give*

Address: *Suite 209*

    Fax: *(813) 257-2141*

        #1 City Center

    E-Mail:

        Palatka, Ind. 27604

Case Style: *Ridges v. AMP Corp. et al.*

- ☐ **Plaintiff (Pros., Pet.)**
- ☒ **Defendant**
- ☐ **Amicus Curia**
- ☐ **Court Appointed**

Facts:

2/1/98   *On March 15, 1996 Mr. Ridges was seated in the driver's seat of his vehicle when an AMP Corp. delivery truck ran into the rear of Mr. Ridges vehicle. Mr. Ridges claims his head was snapped back, then forward causing a concussion. He claims that subsequently he has suffered cognitive defects, memory loss, depression, and post-traumatic stress disorder.*

To Do	Schedule
1. Review records	• Jan–Feb
2. Oral report of review	• Post 1
3. Examination of Mr. Ridges	• Feb–Mar
4. Oral report of results	• Post 3
5. Written Report	• Post 4

Hypothetical Questions:

1. *Does Mr. Ridges suffer cognitive, neurophysical deficits?*
2. *If so—to what extent is he disabled?*
3. *Does Mr. Ridges suffer any other psychological defects?*
4. *If 1, 2, or 3 are found, what are the likeliest proximate*
5. *If 1, 2, or 3 are found, what treatment would be recommended?*

Fees: **Ret:** *$4000.00*

        Dr: *400.00/hr.*

        Tr: *100.00/hr.*

        Res: *50.00/hr.*

- ☒ **Discuss Fee Structure**
- ☒ **Request Initial Letter**
  - • **Designate as consultant**
  - • **Fees pd. on 30-day basis**
  - • **Will send agreement letter**
- ☒ **Suggest Retrieval of Records and Information**
- ☐ **Discuss Pretrial Meeting**
- ☐ **Confirming Letter Received**
- ☐ **First Appointment Scheduled**
- ☒ **CV Sent**

Anticipated Trial Date:

Judge:

Court:

Asst/Secy to Attorney:

Additional:

Form 2   Charge Sheet

Page _____

Case: _____   No.: _____

Date	Staff Person	Function	Time	Amount

Form 2a   Charge Sheet

Case: _Ridges v. AMP (John Surridge, Esq.)_ **No.** _L-1293_

Date	Staff Person	Function	Time	Amount
2-1-98	DR	Initial intake—Telephone conference with Mr. Surridge	1/2	$ 200
2-10-98	DR	Initial review of records sent by Mr. Surridge	3	1200
2-15-98	DR	Continuing review of records sent by Mr. Surridge	2	800
2-20-98	DR	Continuing review of records sent by Mr. Surridge	4	1600
2-22-98	DR	Telephone report of review of records	1	400
3-7-98	DR	Initial interview with Mr. Ridges—History	1 1/2	600
3-8-98	DR	Interview with Mrs. Ridges (wife)	1	400
3-9-98	DR	Telephone interviews—Former supervisor, co-workers	2 1/2	1000
3-14-98	DR	Initial testing of Mr. Ridges	3	1200
3-15-98	CQ	Testing continued with psychometrist	6	600
3-16-98	CQ	Testing continued with psychometrist	4	400
3-18-98	DR	Analysis of test data and conclusions	3	1200
3-19-98	DR	Oral report of results to Mr. Surridge	1	400
3-19-98	DR	Written report sent to Mr. Surridge	—	—
3-20-98	CQ	Initial billing invoice	—	9800
3-20-98	CQ	Minus retainer received 2/9/98	—	(4000)
3-20-98	—	Balance (billed 3-20-98)	—	5800
3-27-98	—	Check received for $5800 from Mr. Surridge. Balance $0		0
5-15-98	DR	Deposition: Called by T. R. Leark, Esq. (bill Mr. Leark)	2	400
6-10-98	DR	Pre-trial conference with Mr. Surridge	1	400
6-25-98	—	Check from Mr. Leark ($400) and check from Mr. Surridge ($400). Balance $0		0
7-2-98	—	Case settled before trial (call from Mr. Surridge)	—	—

1.9

Form 3 Terms of Agreement Letter

_____
[Date]

_____
[Name]

_____
[Address]

Re: Engagement as Expert

Dear Counselor:

Thank you for retaining me to serve as an expert in connection with [Case Name]. My professional services will involve consulting with you and possibly conducting psychological evaluations in the referenced litigation. I hope that my work in this matter will lead to a mutually satisfactory relationship with you.

The purpose of this letter is to confirm my engagement as an expert and to provide you with information concerning my fees, billing, and collection policies as well as other terms that will govern our relationship. I have found it a helpful practice to confirm with my clients the nature and terms of the arrangement.

My engagement as an expert began on [Date], the date on which I was first contacted by [Attorney's Name], regarding this matter. Our engagement will be terminated at will by either of us, subject to payment of all fees for services performed and costs advanced through the date of termination. All payments should be made by the retaining attorney and not directly by the attorney's client or other third party.

Attached to this letter is a summary of my standard terms of engagement for services as an expert. Please review these policies and let me know if you have any questions.

I require a retainer in the amount of $[Amount] against which initial billings will be made. Fees for my personal time spent on this case will be billed at $[Amount] per hour. Should examinations be required test room time is billed at $[Amount] per hour.

If the terms described above and in the attached summary are satisfactory to you, please so indicate by signing the enclosed copy of this letter and returning the signed copy to me.

Again, if you have any questions at all concerning the information contained in this letter or the attached summary, I would be pleased to hear from you.

I am grateful for the opportunity to be able to work with you and your firm in connection with these matters. I look forward to hearing from you.

Sincerely yours,

_____
[Name]

Approved: _____ [Date] _____

By: _____ [Name] _____

Form 4   Terms of Engagement Contract

I appreciate your decision to retain me as your expert. My engagement is limited to the matter identified and the letter to which these terms of engagement are attached. The following summarizes my office's billing practices and certain other terms that will apply to our engagement:

1. We send our bills [monthly/weekly] throughout the engagement for a particular matter. Statements are due when rendered. In instances in which we represent more than one attorney with respect to a matter, each person that we represent is jointly and severally liable for my fees with respect to the representation. My statements contain a concise summary of each matter for which professional services were rendered and a fee was charged.

2. When establishing fees for services I render, I am guided primarily by the time and labor required. I require a retainer in an amount which is appropriate with respect to the proposed professional tasks. Unless otherwise agreed, the retainer will be applied to the last statement rendered in connection with the professional work, with any unused portion being returned to the client.

3. I invite my clients to discuss freely with me any questions that may arise concerning a fee charge for any matter. I want my clients to be satisfied with both the quality of my professional services and the reasonableness of the fees that I charge for these services. I will attempt to provide as much detailed billing information as may be required in any customary form desired. I am willing to discuss with my clients any of the billing formats my office uses and that may best suit the client's needs.

In determining a reasonable fee for the time and labor required for a particular project, I take into account the skills, time demands, and other factors influencing the professional responsibility required for each matter. My internal allocation of values for my time as well as for my psychological assistant, research assistant, and other personnel changes periodically to account for increases in cost of delivering professional services and other economic factors.

Services based on hourly rates are applied perspectively as well as to unbilled time previously expended. My office records and bills time in one-quarter hour (15-minute) increments.

In addition to my professional fees, my statements may include out-of-pocket expenses that my office has advanced on behalf of the client or the client's project.

During the course of my service, it may be appropriate or necessary to hire third parties to provide services on behalf of the project. These services may include such things as consultation with other experts, psychological assistants, or research assistants.

If my statements are not paid within 30 days after they are rendered, I reserve the right to discontinue services until the account is brought current. Additionally, if my statement has not been paid within 30 days from the date of the statement, I automatically impose an interest charge of 1.25 percent per month (15 percent annual percentage rate) from the 30th day after the day of the statement until it is paid in full. Interest charges apply to specific statements on an individual statement basis. Any payments made on past due statements are applied first to the oldest outstanding element. I am entitled to attorney's fees and costs if collection activities are necessary.

I will provide my services as an expert in accordance with the engagement letter that accompanies this attachment. You will provide me with such factual information and materials as I require to perform the services identified in the engagement letter. I will keep you advised of developments as necessary to ensure the timely, effective, and efficient completion of my work.

Regarding the ethics of my profession that will govern my behavior, several points deserve emphasis. As a matter of professional responsibility, I am required to preserve the confidence and secrets of my clients as well as my patients. This obligation and the legal privilege for our communications exist to encourage candid and complete communication. I can perform truly beneficial services for a client only if I am aware of all information that might be relevant to my work as an expert. Consequently, I trust that our relationship with you will be based on mutual confidence and unrestrained communication that will facilitate my proper service to you.

I may be (and sometimes am) asked to represent a client with respect to interests that are adverse to those of another client who I represent in connection with another matter. During the term of this agreement, I agree that I will not accept representation of another client to pursue interests that are directly adverse to your interests unless and until I have made full disclosure to you of all the relevant facts, circumstances, and implications of my undertaking two representations and you have consented to my representation of the other client. In turn, you agree that you will be reasonable in evaluating such circumstances and you will give your consent if we can confirm to you in good faith that the following criteria are met:

1. There is no substantial relationship between any matter in which I am serving you and the matter for the other client.

2. My delivery of professional services to the other client will not implicate any confidential information that I have received from you.

3. My work for you and the discharge of my professional responsibilities to you will not be prejudiced by the other client for the other client has also consented in writing based on full disclosure of the relevant facts, circumstances, and implications of my undertaking the two representations.

By making this agreement, we are establishing the criteria that will govern the exercise of your right under applicable ethical rules to withhold consent to my representation of another client whose interest is adverse to yours. You will retain the right, of course, to contest in good faith my representation that the criteria have been met, in which event I would have the burden of supporting my representation to you.

Upon completion of the matter to which this agreement applies, or upon earlier termination of our relationship, the relationship will end unless you and I have expressly agreed to continuation with respect to other matters. The representation is terminable at will by either party subject to ethical restraints and the payment of all fees and costs.

Your agreement to this engagement constitutes your acceptance of the foregoing terms and conditions. If any of them is unacceptable to you, please advise me now so that we can resolve any differences and proceed with a clear, complete, and consistent understanding of our relationship.

Form 5   Case Chronology

Case: _____   No.: _____

Date	Contact	Time

Form 5a   Case Chronology

Case: _Ridges v. AMP (Mr. Surridge)_   **No.:** _L-1293_

Date	Contact	Time
2-1-98	Intake conference by telephone with Mr. Surridge	8:30 A.M.
2-10-98	Review of records	9:00 A.M.–12:00 P.M.
2-15-98	Review of records	8:00–10:00 A.M.
2-20-98	Review of records	8:00 A.M.–12:00 P.M.
2-22-98	Telephone conference with Mr. Surridge—Summary of records	11:00 A.M.–12:00 P.M.
2-23-98	Schedule first appointment—Mr. Ridges	2:30 P.M.
2-24-98	Schedule first appointment—Mrs. Ridges	9:00 A.M.
3-6-98	Call to remind Mr. & Mrs. Ridges of appointments. Directions given.	9:00 A.M.

Form 6 Case Material Received

Date	Material	Rec'd By

Form 6a Case Material Received

Date	Material	Rec'd By
2-10-98	Medical and psychological reports received from Mr. Surridge	CQ
2-16-98	Raw test data received from Stephen Queen, Ph.D.	DR
3-7-98	Medical records brought by Mr. Ridges	DR
5-1-98	Subpoena received for deposition set for 5-15	CQ

Form 7   Case Materials Sent

Date	Material	Sent By

Form 7a   Case Materials Sent

Date	Material	Sent By
3-19-98	Report of examination of Mr. Ridges to Mr. S.	CQ
4-17-98	Raw test data sent to Stephen Queen, Ph.D.	CQ

Form 8   Forensic Intake Sheet (Pre-Examination)

Case: _____   Date: _____

Name: _____   Status: _____

Current Address: _____

DOB: _____ Age: _____ Education: _____   Telephone: _____

Closest Relative: _____   Relationship: _____

Address: _____   Telephone: _____

Attorney's Name: _____   Telephone: _____

Address: _____   Fax/E-mail: _____

Retaining Attorney for This Case: _____

Appointments Scheduled:

Date	Time	Purpose

Appointments Confirmed On: _____   By: _____

Appointment Card Sent: _____   By: _____

Telephone Reminder On: _____   By: _____

1.19

Form 8a   Forensic Intake Sheet (Pre-Examination)

Case: _Ridges v. AMP Corp._   **Date:** _3-1-98_

Name: _Ridges, John P._   **Status:** _Plaintiff_

Current Address: _132 Elm Street, Palatka, IN 27602_

DOB: _3-5-60_   **Age:** _38-0_   **Education:** _12 (Grad)_   **Telephone:** _969-2102_

Closest Relative: _Mrs. Irma Ridges_   **Relationship:** _Wife_

Address: _Same as above_   **Telephone:** _Same as above_

Attorney's Name: _T. R. Leark, Esq._   **Telephone:** _927-6003_

Address: _2362 Forsyth Ave., Palatka, IN 27612_   **Fax/E-mail:** _927-2121_

Retaining Attorney for This Case: _John Surridge, Esq._

Appointments Scheduled:

Date	Time	Purpose
3-9-98	9:00 A.M.	Initial interview—Mr. R. & Testing.
3-10-98	8:30 A.M.	Initial interview—Mrs. R.
3-11-98	8:30 A.M.	Continued testing of Mr. R.
3-12-98	9:00 A.M.	Continued testing of Mr. R.
3-17-98	9:00 A.M.	Continued testing of Mr. R.

Appointments Confirmed On: _3-6-98_   **By:** _Mrs. Ridges_

Appointment Card Sent: _3-1-98_   **By:** _CQ_

Telephone Reminder On: _3-6-98 & 3-13-98_   **By:** _CQ_

Form 9　Preselection Interview Form

Name: _____　Date: _____

Position Applied For: _____

Why do you want to work in this profession? (use the back of this form)

_____

_____

		Circle Response

Have you ever seen the inside of a jail? How many times? _____　Yes　No

I.　School

A.　What is the highest level of education you have obtained?

_____

B.　Were you involved in any school or after-school activities? Which ones?　Yes　No

_____

C.　Have you ever been suspended or expelled from school?　Yes　No

_____

D.　Were you in any special classes or placement? Which ones?　Yes　No

_____

II.　Work

A.　Are you working now? Where?　Yes　No

_____

B.　Have you ever had problems with your boss/coworkers?　Yes　No

_____

C.　Have you ever been disciplined at a previous job? How many times?　Yes　No

_____

D.　Have you ever been fired or asked to leave a job? How many times?　Yes　No

_____

E.　What is the longest time you ever held a job?

_____

F.　How many jobs have you had in the past two years? List and indicate the approximate number of months employed at each.

_____

III.　Military

A.　Have you been in the military? _____　Yes　No

B.　What was your last rank? _____

C.　Conditions of discharge? _____

D.　Were your disciplined? How many times?　Yes　No

_____

IV. Social

    A. Do you have any hobbies?   Yes   No

    _____

    B. How do you spend your spare time?

    _____

    C. Do you exercise?   Yes   No

    _____

    D. Do you or your spouse have any past-due credit accounts?   Yes   No

    _____

    E. Have you ever been told you have a problem with your temper?   Yes   No

    _____

V. Law

    A. Have you ever had any felony convictions?   Yes   No

    _____

    B. Have you ever committed a crime?   Yes   No

    _____

    C. How many vehicle code violations have you received (number of tickets)?

    _____

    D. How many fistfights or shoving matches have you been in?

    _____

    E. When was your last fistfight?

    _____

    F. Have you ever used a weapon in a fight?   Yes   No

    _____

VI. Addictive Behavior

    A. Do you or have you ever used illegal drugs?   Yes   No

    _____

    B. Have you ever smoked marijuana without other people?   Yes   No

    _____

    C. Have you ever smoked marijuana more than one time in a week?   Yes   No

    _____

    D. Do you consume alcohol?   Yes   No

        1. How many drinks do you have per week? _____

        2. How often do you get intoxicated? _____

        3. When do you get intoxicated? _____

        4. Have you ever been violent while drinking?   Yes   No

        _____

        5. Have you ever been in an accident while drinking?   Yes   No

        _____

        6. Have you ever been told that you have a drinking problem?   Yes   No

        _____

VII. Physical Health

    A. Do you have any physical limitations or problems?   Yes   No

    _____

    B. List serious physical ailments and approximate time they occurred.

    _____

    C. Are you taking any medication?   Yes   No
       What medication? _____
       For what purpose? _____

VIII. Mental Health

    A. Are you or have you ever been in counseling or therapy?   Yes   No
       For what? _____
       How long? _____

    B. What are your bad habits and faults?

    _____

    C. What are your good habits and assets?

    _____

    D. Have you ever been hospitalized for mental, nervous, or stress problems?   Yes   No

    _____

    E. Have you ever taken medication for your "nerves" or for a mental
       condition?   Yes   No

    _____

    F. Do you experience any of the following conditions?   Yes   No

(Check the appropriate column)

	None	Rarely	Less Than Average	More Than Average	Frequently	Always
1. Pain	___	___	___	___	___	___
2. Lack of energy	___	___	___	___	___	___
3. Suicidal thoughts	___	___	___	___	___	___
4. Poor memory	___	___	___	___	___	___
5. Expressing too much or too little anger	___	___	___	___	___	___
6. Problems concentrating	___	___	___	___	___	___
7. Financial problems	___	___	___	___	___	___
8. Dizziness	___	___	___	___	___	___
9. Family problems	___	___	___	___	___	___
10. Feelings of being misunderstood	___	___	___	___	___	___
11. Nervousness	___	___	___	___	___	___
12. Fear	___	___	___	___	___	___
13. Stress	___	___	___	___	___	___
14. Sadness	___	___	___	___	___	___
15. Eating problems	___	___	___	___	___	___
16. Sleeping problems	___	___	___	___	___	___
17. Anxiety in closed or dark places	___	___	___	___	___	___
18. Problems getting along w/certain "types of people"	___	___	___	___	___	___
19. Feeling overwhelmed	___	___	___	___	___	___
20. Difficulty remaining calm	___	___	___	___	___	___

IX. Other

    A. Is there anything else that you feel should be known, positive or negative, that might have an impact on your application or possible employment, if discovered later?

    _____

    B. Is there anything that was unclear or would you like to change your response to any question?

    _____

    C. I have answered all questions honestly and to the best of my ability.
    I consent and understand that the information I provided may be used to assist in determining my application/employment status.
    I further understand that intentional misstatements or false information could result in the denial or termination of my application.

    _____   _____

    Signature   Date

Chapter 2

Initiating the Assessment Process

FORM 10
Background Summary—
From Record Review

This form summarizes important elements that the psychologist finds in reading the record before the psychological examination. It may be used for a handy reference for a variety of reasons including sending for previous records.

Form 10   Background Summary—From Record Review

Name: _____   Date: _____

1. Elementary School: _____

2. Jr. High School: _____

3. High School: _____

4. Other: _____

5. Previous Psychological Tests: _____

   _____

   _____

6. Previous Accidents, Injuries, Poisoning:

   _____

7. Unconsciousness:

   _____

8. Medication Now:

   _____

   _____

9. Previous Traumatic Experiences: _____

10. Memory
   A. Recent   _____
   B. Past   _____
   C. Pre-Event   _____
   D. Post-Event _____

Form 10a   Background Summary—From Record Review

Name: _Ridges, John_   Date: _3-1-98_

1. Elementary School: _Palatka Elem. 9-66 (Repeats 3rd)_
2. Jr. High School: _Wilson Middle 9-74_
3. High School: _Plant 9-77—Graduated 6-81. Vocational Courses_
4. Other: _Air Conditioning Training_
5. Previous Psychological Tests: _Elementary 10-68_
   High School 4-79
   U.S. Army 10-81

6. Previous Accidents, Injuries, Poisoning:

   Football, 1980. Momentary "Blackout." No medical Rx.

7. Unconsciousness:

   _No_

8. Medication Now:

   Tylenol

   Xanax (Dr. Jones) 0.25 T.I.D.

9. Previous Traumatic Experiences: _No_

10. Memory
    A. Recent   _Claims poor_
    B. Past   _Claims poor_
    C. Pre-Event   _No problem_
    D. Post-Event _Variable_

Chapter 3

Initiating a
Forensic Evaluation

FORM 11
Apprisal of Rights

Informed consent is a necessary preliminary to almost all psychological services. It is crucial in forensic work. Litigation is involved in most forensic work done by psychologists and the potential for lawsuits is higher than for ordinary professional activity.

Form 11 is an informed consent document that can be used before conducting a psychological examination of an adult referred by an agency. This form specifically states that the results are *not* privileged. Form 11a shows how this form is used when the referral is from a judge. Form 11b is this informed consent form in Spanish.

FORM 12
Authorization for Release of
Psychological Information

During the course of a forensic case, the psychologist is likely to receive requests or subpoenas for records in the psychologist's files. Form 12 is an authorization to release specific information about an individual. Form 12a is a completed request asking for the individual's psychological report and raw test data to be sent to a psychologist with whom the individual has begun treatment. When the individual is a minor, there's a place for the parents' signature.

FORM 13
Authorization for Release or
Receipt of Information

Form 13 is an authorization to either receive or to send information. It includes a list of applicable state standards and a liability disclaimer. This form should be modified to include the appropriate state statute numbers.

FORM 14
Psychological Evaluation
Informed Consent

Form 14 is to be read and signed by the individual who is to be tested. The form tells the individual what is going to take place, encouraging the individual to feel free to communicate any discomfort to the examiner.

Forensic evaluations frequently include measures of validity, deception, or symptom exaggeration. This informed consent advises the test taker of this as a "fair warning."

Form 11   Apprisal of Rights

Name of Examinee: _____

Date(s) of Examination: _____

This psychological examination to be conducted by _____[Name]_____ was scheduled at the
request of _____[Name]_____.

This agency retained _____[Name]_____ for this examination. The examination will consist of
questions and psychological tests. These will be used by _____[Name]_____ to write a psychological
report for the agency requesting this examination. The information in this report may be used against me.
The report and the tests will be available to my attorney(s).

This statement has been read to me and I understand it. I understand I have the right to consult with my
attorney if I have any questions about this.

Signed: _____

Examiner: _____

Date: _____

Witness: _____

Date: _____

Form 11a   Appraisal of Rights

Name of Examinee: _John P. Thomas_

Date(s) of Examination: _January 8, 1988_

This psychological examination to be conducted by _James Kaufman, Ph.D._ was scheduled at the request of _Jane Algood, Chief Counselor, Child and Family Protection Team_.

This agency retained _____Dr. Kaufman_____ for this examination. The examination will consist of questions and psychological tests. These will be used by _____Dr. Kaufman_____ to write a psychological report for the agency requesting this examination. The information in this report may be used against me. The report and the tests will be available to my attorney(s).

This statement has been read to me and I understand it. I understand I have the right to consult with my attorney if I have any questions about this.

Signed: _____

Examiner: _____

Date: ___1-8-98_____

Witness: _____

Date: _1-8-98_____

Form 11b   Aviso de Derechos

Nombre del Examindado: _____

Fecha del Examen: _____

Este examen psicológico, el cual sera conducido por _____ fue fijado a petición de _____.

Esta agencia empleó _____ para conducir este examen. El examen consistirá a la vez de preguntas y pruebas psicológicas. Basándose en estos datos _____ escribirá un informe psicológico para la agencia que ha pedido este examen. Los conocimientos contenidos en este informe podran ser usados en contra mía. El informe y las pruebas seran puestas a la disposición de mi abogado(s).

Me han leído esta declaración y yo la comprendo. Si tengo alguna duda acerca de esto, entiendo que yo tengo el derecho de consultar con mi abogado.

Firmdado: _____

Examindador: _____

Fecha: _____

Testigo: _____

Fecha: _____

Form 12   Authorization for Release of Psychological Information

Regarding: _____   DOB: _____

To: _____

I, _____, hereby consent and authorize you to release specified information concerning the above named individual to:

      __ [Name] _____

      __ [Address] _____

      _____

The information shall include, _____

_____

I understand that I may revoke this consent at anytime except to the extent that action based on this consent has already been taken. This informed consent for the release of information will automatically expire without further action ninety days after the date on which it was signed.

I hereby release _____ from all legal responsibility that may arise from the release of the above requested information. This authorization is fully understood and it is made voluntarily and with informed consent on my part.

_____   _____
[Signature]   [Witness]

_____   _____
[Signature of Parent/Guardian]   [Date]

_____
[Date]

Form 12a   Authorization for Release of Psychological Information

Regarding: _Jane P. Doe_   DOB: _6-17-65_

To: _Daryl Raines, Ph.D._

I, _Jane P. Doe_, hereby consent and authorize you to release specified information concerning the above named individual to:

          Mary Brown, Ph.D.

           23 Elm St. Suite 2-B

           Templeton, Illiana

The information shall include, _Report of testing and raw test data_

I understand that I may revoke this consent at anytime except to the extent that action based on this consent has already been taken. This informed consent for the release of information will automatically expire without further action ninety days after the date on which it was signed.

I hereby release _Dr. Raines_ from all legal responsibility that may arise from the release of the above requested information. This authorization is fully understood and it is made voluntarily and with informed consent on my part.

Jane P. Doe	_Mary Doe_
[Signature]	[Witness]

William P. Doe	_3-13-98_
[Signature of Parent/Guardian]	[Date]

_3-13-98_
[Date]

Form 13 Authorization for Release or Receipt of Information

Regarding (Name): _____

Social Security No.: _____ DOB: _____ Date: _____

This will authorize [Examiner's Name] to release/receive general medical, psychological/psychiatric information including alcohol/drug abuse or addiction from my health records in accordance with [State] Statutes and [State] and Federal Administrative Rules and Regulations to/from:

_____

_____

Information to Be   [   ]   Released   [   ]   Received Is as Follows:
[   ]   Histories and Physicals   [   ]   Psychological Testing Raw Data
[   ]   Reports of Psychological Testing   [   ]   Hospital Discharge Summary
[   ]   Office Notes
[   ]   Other _____

Purpose of Release:
[   ]   Continued Treatment   [   ]   Other _____
[   ]   Psychological/Neuropsychological Evaluation

Release Duration:
[   ]   One Time   [   ]   Continuous for 90 days

Notice of Prohibition on Redisclosure: This information has been disclosed to you from records protected by Federal Rules governing confidentiality rules (42 CFR Part 2) and [State] Statutes: [   ]. The Federal Rules and State Statutes prohibit making further disclosure of this information without the specific written consent of the person to whom it pertains or as otherwise permitted by 42 CFR Part 2.

I understand that I have the right to refuse to sign this authorization and that the facility named above is released from all legal liability that may arise from the release of the information requested. Consent is subject to revocation at any time except to the extent that the action based on this consent has already been taken. This authorization for release will automatically expire without further action 90 days after the date on which it was signed.

_____   _____
            [Signature]   [Date]

_____   _____
[Signature of Empowered Representative   [Witness]
(If patient is unable to sign)

Form 14   Psychological Evaluation Informed Consent

We have scheduled a psychological evaluation for: ___[Name]_____

The evaluation will take place: Day: _____   Date: _____   Time: _____

Day: _____   Date: _____   Time: _____

Day: _____   Date: _____   Time: _____

Day: _____   Date: _____   Time: _____

During the course of the evaluation, you will have interviews, you will take standardized psychological tests, and observations will be made of your responses. These procedures are standardized and will take place under specific testing conditions.

We urge you to do your best. If for any reason you do not feel that you can do your best, please inform us so that we can stop the evaluation and reschedule at a time that you are likely to feel more comfortable.

If you become tired during the course of the evaluation, please do not hesitate to tell us so that you can be given an opportunity to stretch, walk around, or to take a break. Please let us know if you become hungry, thirsty, sleepy, or in any way uncomfortable.

Built-in to these tests are measurements of validity and cooperation. It is very important that you do your best with an understanding that these various validity measures will identify uncooperative, inconsistent, or purposely distorted responses.

We will make every effort to have your evaluation be a comfortable one and ensure as best we can that the results will be helpful for you.

I understand all of the above and I am willing to proceed as indicated.

_____   _____
[Examinee's Signature]   [Witness]

Chapter 4

Process Forms

FORM 15
Informed Consent—Child Custody/Visitation Evaluation

Form 15 is an informed consent form to be used before conducting an evaluation of a divorced family. In the example provided on Form 15a, the divorced couple is returning to court as a result of the father's petition to increase his visitation time with the children. The mother opposes this. The judge has requested a psychological evaluation of the parents and both children before he renders a decision in this matter.

This form ensures that both parents have agreed to the evaluation and that the psychologist is "held harmless" or immune to future litigation by the parents regarding the evaluations.

FORM 16
Informed Consent—Custody and Visitation Evaluation

Form 16 is another informed consent agreement that is appropriate where the evaluation is to be done with single parents or with stepparents in a blended family situation. In the example presented on Form 16a, the stepfather, husband of the biological mother grants permission for the evaluation.

FORMS 17–21
Informed Consent and Permission Forms

Forms 17 through 20 present informed consent and permission forms that may be used as alternates to the previously presented forms. Form 21 is a permission form to allow the psychologist to contact other professionals, agencies, or schools requesting information about the individual.

FORM 22
Family History—Child

Form 22 allows the clinician to question the family about the child. It is a coded form, helping the clinician to carry the family through a good many areas of the child's development. Page one of this form allows clinician to ask for the name, age, occupation, education, health, and personality characteristics for all of the adult family members. It also leaves space to record what the family has to say about sibling relationships. There is a space for "others" to record the child's contact with grandparents, uncles, aunts, or caregivers. The family's socioeconomic level can be indicated on this page. Clinician may ask about the kinds of things that the father does when interacting with the child and the same for the mother. The family can be asked as to the "climate" of the home—whether it is an easygoing setting or the parents like things "just so." There is a space for the clinician to put down observations as to the character and response style of the parents.

Page two records details of the child's early growth and development. Starting with birthdate and age, it moves on to the conditions of the birth, the feeding pattern, when toilet training began, the degree to which the child navigated the first year, and how satisfied the parents were with the years two through five. The form allows the parents to indicate the child's primary physician, whether the child had any medical procedures such as a tonsillectomy and adenoidectomy. The usual childhood diseases are recorded here as well as information about immunization. On this form, the parents can be asked about regular complaints of the child, whether puberty has begun, and whether sex education has been given and the nature of this. Toward the end of the form, there is an opportunity to record information that may relate to the neuropsychological development of the child, such as the occurrence of unconsciousness, high fevers, seizures, dizziness, headaches, or mixed cerebral dominance in the family chain.

Some indication of the child's contact and relationship with grandparents and religion can be indicated on this sheet. Any traumas the child has suffered, such as being lost, kidnapped, or abused should be recorded here.

The form then leads the clinician to question the parents about the child's school, friendships, and the conditions of the home. The clinician asks whether the child has his or her own room, recreational activities, relations with siblings, eating habits, discipline style for the family, whether the child has been to camp—day or overnight—sporting activities the child enjoys, any hobbies the child may have, and in the case of adolescents, their dating behavior. The clinician can ask about allowance, the usual bedtime during school hours and any chores that the child may have. There is a place to record whether the child has generally performed below potential in the school setting as well as whether the child has been socially embarrassing. Some indication as to whether the child has homework and how this is handled in the home can be noted.

Page four is a chart that can be filled out concerning common behaviors of children, when they started, whether they continue, and any other comments concerning these matters.

FORM 23
Adult History

These four pages are a structured history form similar to that presented for children in Form 22, but for an adult. This set of structured sheets gives the clinician an opportunity to record significant data during the first interview with the individual being evaluated. The first page allows for a description of current complaints, specific symptoms, and what the individual hopes is going to happen in the future. Any questions the individual has may be recorded here. Under "Greatest stress," the clinician may put down additional material that is important in understanding the subject's current status.

Page two allows for basic information such as the parent figures, whether they're living, well, deceased, and their ages and occupations. Siblings, grandparents, and significant others in the life of the subject may be described here. There is space to put down the individual's religious preferences. The clinician can record the subject's description of family conflicts, what the subject was like during growth and developmental years, and the subject's academic and vocational history. Whether the individual was in the military service and the subject's record in the criminal justice system can be identified here.

The third page of the form allows the clinician to indicate medical information, any early experience that might have caused neurological damage, and the subject's habitual use of licit and illicit substances. The bottom half of this sheet allows the clinician to record information concerning the subject's sexual history.

The final page of this form is for the clinician to record information that is helpful in understanding the subject's social, cultural, and leisure time life. An opportunity to question the subject about marriage and current marital situation completes the form.

Form 23a is filled out for a 32-year-old male, indicted for income tax evasion, embezzlement, and commercial fraud. The defense attorney is claiming that Mr. Jones is incompetent to stand trial. The judge has requested psychological evaluation to help in making a determination in this case.

FORM 24
Test Room Schedule

This form allows the clinician to schedule the testing in a forensic case. Aside from basic information plus the appointment times, it is a list of all of the tests and procedures that are available so that the clinician can plan the assessment.

Form 24a shows a test room schedule that has been filled out for Timothy Jones, the individual whose history form was presented on Form 23. Each of the procedures that will be conducted is marked with an X. Some of the testing will be done by the doctor. The history will be done by the doctor. The nine hours in the test room will be divided between the doctor and the psychological assistant.

On this form the history, the interview and the clinical observations as well as WAIS-III Comprehension and Digit Span were administered by the doctor. The doctor also administered the Structured

Interview of Reported Symptoms and the Wisconsin Card Sort. These are marked accordingly so that when the doctor gives the deposition he can clearly state which procedures were done by him and which were done by the psychological assistant. In addition, the doctor administered the Rorschach examination and portions of the clinical observations.

When a procedure is finished the X will be circled. Where no circle exists, that procedure is yet to be done.

In this case, a fairly thorough evaluation of intellect, neuropsychological status, reading skills, competency for trial, and personality are covered. In addition, several tests of validity or "faking bad" were included.

There is a space called "Workup" that will be filled in after the psychologist has all of the tests and constructs the written report. This allows the clinician to have one place where he or she can respond to the question of how much time was spent on the case and for what purposes.

On the top left of the form there are spaces for "XIT #1 and #2." This is where the clinician would mark down the dates for interpretation of the results if there is going to be an oral interpretation. This is relatively rare in forensic work. On Form 24a, it is marked "Report to Ass't. U.S. Attorney Cates" indicating there will be no oral report but simply a written report forwarded to the U.S. Attorney and to the judge.

FORM 25
Family Conference

The family conference form is a single sheet that allows the clinician to put down information that arises from a conference with either family members or other important individuals in the subject's life. It can be used to record information during a telephone conference with an employer, a relative, or a teacher. In the case presented on Form 25a, this form was used as part of the evaluation of a 15-year-old boy who had been in a serious motor vehicle accident approximately a year before the interview took place.

FORM 26
Neuropsychological
Symptom/Sign/Course

Form 26 is the material referred to on Form 25a as the Neuropsychological Symptom/Sign/Course form. Form 26a presents this form filled out after interviewing the mother, the father, and the uncle. This form can also be filled out after interviewing teachers or employers to determine the consistency between relatives' reports and the reports of more objective observers.

FORM 27
Posttraumatic Stress Disorder
Checklist and Interview

This four-page form is provided for subjects who are claiming Posttraumatic Stress Disorder as a result of some event for which they seek remedy in the courts. The first page is a summary of the reported symptoms or conditions according to the *Diagnostic and Statistical Manual of Mental Disorders-IV (DSM-IV)* of the American Psychiatric Association. Pages two through four allow the clinician to ask the individual for details concerning each of the possible symptoms. After filling out pages two, three, and four, the clinician will use the first page as a checklist to demonstrate the subject's report of the symptoms associated with Posttraumatic Stress Disorder.

Because this is a self-report instrument, it is subject to questions concerning reliability and validity. It is useful for a comparison of the subject's view of himself or herself and the objective test finding that will be found in the full psychological evaluation.

FORM 28
Drug Use History

This form is useful in working with subjects who may be using their drug background to exculpate themselves from specific intent. Although intoxication does not result in criminal behavior being excused, it can sometimes be the difference between a first-degree felony and a lesser charge if specific intent is proven to have been absent.

Form 28a demonstrates the use of this form with a 38-year-old incarcerated subject who is accused of murder, and will be pleading intoxication as part of a defense strategy.

FORM 29
Medications

This form is useful in cases where an individual is taking medications that may have some effect on either their behavior or accountability in criminal or civil issues such as competence. The form provides an opportunity for the clinician to identify the source of the information (including reading the material from medical records or from the actual medication containers). The form allows for identification of the medication, the dosage, the physician who prescribed it, and the purpose of the medication. In forensic cases, the clinician is often asked what medications the subject is taking or has been taking.

FORM 30
Clinical Observations

This form allows the clinician (and his or her assistant where appropriate) to make notations about the observable behavior of the subject either during interview or during testing. The clinician may note the subject's behavior in the waiting room. This form will be the basis for a descriptive paragraph that is a usual and customary part of a clinical report.

FORM 31
Assessment Time Log

During the course of a forensic case, either during deposition or at the trial itself while the expert is giving testimony, one attorney or another may well ask the psychologist when he or she saw the subject, how much time was spent with the subject, and what portion of the assessment was done by the psychologist. Form 31 is an opportunity for the psychologist to keep a very accurate record of how much time he or she spent with the subject, what was done, and the time spent with the subject by psychological assistants.

Form 31a presents an Assessment Time Log Form filled out during the evaluation of a 42-year-old man who is referred for evaluation as to competency to stand trial.

FORM 32
Behavioral Symptomatology of Borderline Personality

This simple checklist allows the clinician to review history and collateral information in order to identify those symptoms that would suggest a subject suffers a Borderline Personality. Rather than being dependent on the *DSM-IV*, this checklist refers to original research that identifies this particular condition. Where more than half of the 21 symptoms are found, the clinician would then move on to *DSM-IV* to determine if the individual met the current standards for a diagnosis of Borderline Personality.

FORM 33
Glasgow Coma Scale and Trauma Score

Form 33 is useful when the psychologist must review records that include emergency medical service or emergency room records in a post head trauma case. Very often the earliest indication of the severity of the head injury is reported in terms of the Glasgow Coma Scale or the Trauma Score.

FORM 34
Items Frequently Used to Access Mental Status in Dementing Patients

Emergency medical service and emergency room personnel often report the cognitive status of an individual with a head injury in terms of their "mental status." Form 34 is a guideline for the interpretation of such commentary that might be on record.

FORM 35
Competency Evaluation Instrument

Although determination of competency may vary from state to state and within the federal sector, Form 35 presents six areas that are generally applicable in most jurisdictions. This is a summary form that the psychologist may use after conducting interviews, reviewing records, and conducting psychological tests. The wording in each of the six subsections is useful in the construction of the final report for the description of what the psychologist found.

FORM 36
Insanity Defense Evaluation

Form 36 is useful when the psychologist is conducting an examination to help the court or either the defense or prosecution to determine whether the subject meets the criteria for "insanity." This checklist ensures that the psychologist has covered all the material that might be useful in making a final report to help in this determination.

FORM 37
Reporting Sanity and
Competence Findings

The material on Form 37 recommends language that a psychologist may use in a report of a sanity evaluation or a competency assessment. This language helps the psychologist to avoid answering the ultimate question that lies in the hands of triers of fact.

FORM 38
Institutional Cost Survey

In the course of conducting forensic work (usually divorce or custody evaluations), the psychologist may be requested to help the parents, or in some cases, the court find a proper institutional placement for a child with learning disabilities or emotional problems. Form 38 provides an opportunity for the psychologist to report the names and facilities as well as the cost for various institutions that might be appropriate for the child.

FORM 39
Clinical Procedures Note

It is important that all clients understand that there are limits to confidentiality and privilege. This is particularly true in forensic work. Form 39 presents a general clinical procedures note that addresses this issue.

FORM 40
Limits of Confidentiality

Form 40 is a similar note that can be given to the patient, and signed by both the psychologist and the subject before any kind of assessment takes place.

FORM 41
Follow-Up Contacts

Form 41 allows the forensic examiner to identify collateral contacts or follow-up contacts that may be had with the subject, family members, teachers, coworkers, or supervisors.

FORM 42
Wechsler Scales—Comparison Sheet

In the course of forensic evaluations, the psychologist may have access to testing results from a previous time in the subject's life. This is particularly valuable in personal injury litigation where the question arises as to how an individual's performance compares with sometime previous to a trauma—emotional or physical.

This form provides an opportunity to compare standard Wechsler scales (Wechsler-Bellevue I and II, Wechsler Adult Intelligence Scale, Wechsler Adult Intelligence Scale-Revised, Wechsler Adult Intelligence Scale III).

Form 42a compares these scales for an adult who suffered a traumatic brain injury. He was given a Wechsler Adult Intelligence Scale during his high school years and a Wechsler Adult Intelligence Scale-Revised at the time of the examination, posttrauma by one year.

FORM 43
Wechsler Scales for Children—
Comparison Sheet

Form 43 is specifically designed to make comparisons on children's Wechsler Scales. Form 43a presents a comparison of a Wechsler Intelligence Scale-Revised given to a youngster during his second grade in school with a Wechsler Intelligence Scale-III given at age 15 one year and three months after a severe motor vehicle accident.

FORM 44
Achievement Tests
Comparison Sheet

Form 44 can be used to make comparisons of achievement test scores on individuals who are being evaluated for the effects of a trauma—physical or emotional—that supposedly has affected their academic work. Form 44a presents such a form filled out for the 15-year-old that was presented in Form 43a.

FORM 45
Testing Comparison Sheet
(Up to Three Wechslers)

Form 45 is useful when a comparison of Wechsler Scales and Subscales involve two or three test administrations, which is more likely to occur where the forensic case involves neuropsychological deficit.

FORM 46
Psychological Autopsy Face Sheet

The validity of the psychological autopsy in determining probable cause of death has been accepted by the courts (see reference, description, and procedures in: Blau, *Psychologist as Expert Witness* 2nd ed., John Wiley, 1998). The Face Sheet provides an opportunity for the clinician to identify the deceased together with some basic data, the specific date of termination, and possible anniversaries in the background that might be associated with the death (termination). This form also allows for a brief description of the circumstances of death as well as a summary of the autopsy report. Form 46a presents a Psychological Autopsy Face Sheet for a 72-year-old woman who was found dead of a gunshot wound. The referral was made to determine whether this was suicide or homicide.

FORM 47
Evaluation of Pre-Terminal Month—
Psychological Autopsy

Form 46 presented a first sheet for recording basic data concerning a death that may have been homicide or suicide. The purpose of the psychological autopsy was to help the law enforcement authorities determine whether they should proceed with a homicide investigation.

After the basic data is developed on Form 46, Form 47 provides an opportunity for the clinician to record significant information from interviews. Interviews should be conducted with any person who has had dealings with the deceased during the month prior to termination. The items to be addressed in the interview as noted on Form 47 are the results of research in psychological autopsies.

Form 47a presents a completed interview with a woman who employed the deceased as a seamstress. She was in the habit of seeing her every week and had known her for over five years.

FORM 48
Psychological Autopsy Interview

Form 48 is an alternate interview form for use in conducting a psychological autopsy.

FORM 49
Final Form for Psychological Autopsy

Form 49 is a final form for the conduct of a psychological autopsy. It is an opportunity for the psychologist to describe the most probable scenario leading up to the termination and the conclusions drawn from all of the interviews and the investigation. Form 49a presents such a form filled out for the individual described in the previous forms.

FORM 50
Visitation Questionnaire

Conducting a custodial or visitation evaluation is a very extensive and complex clinical procedure. It involves the parental partners, the children, and often other relatives. The court looks to the professional person for guidance in making what often turns to be Solomonic decisions. In many instances, there is no painless way for the court to "split the baby." The professional psychologist has an obligation to do as complete an evaluation as possible and to make conservative recommendations that are primarily in the best interests of the child and secondarily in the interests of the often battling parents.

Since most custody and visitation evaluations involve people who are at "war" with each other, they are often seen for separate histories. Form 50 allows the clinician to interview the parent or the parent-surrogate and determine the wishes, attitudes, prejudices, and fears of the potential custodial or visitation figure.

Form 50a was filled out with the mother of two children who is vigorously opposing any visitation by the ex-husband or any member of the ex-husband's family.

FORM 51
The Best Interests of the Child—
Parent Evaluation Worksheet

In preparing a final report on custodial or visitation recommendations, the psychologist will probably conduct a number of interviews and fairly extensive psychological testing to determine where the parental figure meets the best interests of the child and where there are difficulties or barriers. Form 51 allows the psychologist to summarize findings in a number of areas and to do a preliminary outline of information that will appear in the final report. Form 51a presents such a workup sheet for the mother of the two children noted on Form 50.

FORM 52
The Best Interests of the Child—
Workup Sheet

As with the parental figures in a custodial, divorce, or visitation evaluation, the psychologist is quite likely to do extensive observation, interviewing, and testing of each child in the marriage. Since the first order of business is to determine the best interests of the child, this form allows the clinician to make notes concerning key elements of the evaluation. It can also serve as an outline for the material that will be presented in the final report for consideration by the court as well as the families. Form 52a presents a completed workup sheet for one of the children in the custodial case noted on previous forms.

FORM 53
The Best Interests of the Child

This form provides an opportunity for the psychologist to summarize recommendations that emerge from the evaluation of the best interests of the child. The form is a sheet that can be helpful preliminary to writing the final report and recommendations. Form 53a shows how this form may be used in a specific case.

FORM 54
Meeting the Best Interests of the
Children: Parental Summary

This is a form that allows the clinician to summarize the assets and liabilities of each of the parental figures in the life of the child. In preparation for writing the custody or visitation report, this gives the clinician an opportunity all during the assessment to identify things that would be important to mention in the recommendation phase of the report.

Form 54a presents a parental summary for the mother of young "Willie" who appeared on previous forms. This particular form is filled out all during the assessment, and includes history, observations, test results, and interviews.

No matter how difficult the marital situation, the clinician should make every effort to identify as fully as possible the assets as well as the liabilities of each custodial or visitation individual.

FORM 55
Visitation Plan Outline

A visitation or custody planning report is generally a very lengthy piece of work. It includes data that results from a careful evaluation of the family situation. Form 55 presents an outline that can be useful in helping the clinician formulate the raw data into a meaningful report that can be useful not only to the court but to the parents.

FORM 56
Standard Paragraphs for
Custody or Visitation Plan

Form 56 presents some standard paragraphs that can be used at various points in a custody or visitation report. Although the ideas expressed in these paragraphs may seem simplistic to a clinician, they may be "new material" to both the court and the parental figures.

FORM 57
Wisconsin Card Sort—Scoring
and Interpretation

The Wisconsin Card Sort is a standardized element of most neuropsychological batteries. The forensic psychologist may do a neuropsychological evaluation in a variety of civil and criminal cases. Form 57 is a convenient way of summarizing the major scores on the Wisconsin Card Sort and comparing them with standards provided by the test's authors.

Form 57a presents the Wisconsin Card Sort data for a 57-year-old woman who was a victim of a motor vehicle accident in which she was rendered unconscious and remained in a coma for a number of days.

FORM 58
Trails A and B

Form 58 presents a form on which the clinician can compare the performance of the subject on the subtest of the Halstead-Reitan Neuropsychological Battery with the normative references for normals at various age ranges.

Form 58a presents this form filled out for the subject first noted on Form 57a. In this case, as with the Wisconsin Card Sort, the subject's performance is significantly poorer than age-related normative sample that is identified at the bottom of the form.

FORM 59
Hand Dynamometer

This form is another opportunity for the clinician to describe the performance of a subject on a standardized neuropsychological test and to make a comparison with well-established normative data. The value of having the test scores on a single sheet that describes the performance and the significance of the performance is that the information is readily available in the subject's file for purposes of constructing the report, for describing the performance during deposition, or for reference during court testimony.

Form 59a shows this form as used in a case involving an adolescent who received a significant brain injury as a result of a motor vehicle accident. In this instance, the test performance was well within normal limits.

FORM 60
Formulae and Worksheet for Estimating Premorbid WAIS-R Scores

In forensic work, particularly in civil actions involving personal injury, the issue as to whether there has been a decrease in intellectual ability and/or cognitive function as a result of an accident becomes of signal importance. A number of formulae have been developed for estimating the level of intellect that existed previous to the accident. Form 62 presents one formulae for what has been established as a reliable method of calculating these scores. Form 60a is a work sheet that can be used by the clinician in making the calculations.

FORM 61
MMPI Comparison

In the course of many forensic cases, there will be records that include a variety of psychological assessments. Since the Minnesota Multiphasic Personality Inventory is the most commonly used objective personality test, it is likely that subjects who have received previous psychological evaluations will have completed this particular instrument.

Form 61 allows the clinician to have one sheet that illustrates all of the T-scores for the major scales of various MMPIs that have been given to the subject.

FORM 62
Probability of Malingering Checklist

For some years now behavioral science experts have been expected by the courts to render opinions as to *malingering*. A variety of psychological tests and procedures have been developed for the assessment of malingering (deception, dissimulation, faking bad, or exaggeration of symptoms). Form 62 presents a checklist for use by the clinician in a first estimate of whether there is a probability of malingering.

FORM 63
Factors That Increase Potential Incredibility and Distortion in the Testimony of Children

In recent years, children of a younger and younger age have been admitted to the courtroom in both civil and criminal cases. Sometimes the credibility of children is challenged. It is less likely that children will be accused of malingering as much as they will be seen as objects of the manipulative needs of adults, or of limited cognitive capacity. Form 63 presents 20 factors that have been associated in the literature with questionable credibility for the testimony of children.

FORMS 64–68
Scoring Sheets for Various Malingering Indices on a Variety of Psychological Tests

Forms 64 through 68 present convenient scoring sheets for recording various malingering indices from various psychological tests (the Halstead-Reitan Booklet Category Test, the Luria-Nebraska Neuropsychological Battery, the Wechsler Adult Intelligence Scale-Revised, the Wechsler Memory Scale-Revised and the Lees-Haley MMPI-2 Fake Bad Scale). For an in-depth discussion of the use of these indices, see Blau, T. (1998). *The psychologist as expert witness,* 2nd ed. New York: John Wiley & Sons.

Forms 64a through 68a present these various scoring sheets for the case of a woman who is the plaintiff in a personal injury case claiming both neuropsychological and emotional deficit as a result of her accident.

FORM 69
Invalidity/Fake Bad/Exaggeration/ Malingering Profile

This form allows the clinician to summarize the results of a number of validity indices that may be developed during the assessment process. Based on the normative data which is available, as well as clinical judgment, the clinician can estimate the probabilities from 1 to 99 that were found for each of the tests given. These can then be profiled on the form to give a visual picture of the probability that the testing is not a valid indicator of the subject's condition.

Form 69a presents this profile for the case presented on Forms 64 through 68.

Form 15   Informed Consent—Child Custody/ Visitation Evaluation

Parents' Names: (Mother) _____

(Father) _____

(Others) _____

Children: _____ Age: _____

_____ Age: _____

_____ Age: _____

_____ Age: _____

Domiciliary Status: _____

_____

_____

Legal Status: _____

_____

Permission is granted to _____[Examiner]_____ to conduct a psychological

evaluation of: _____ Mother   [Age]_____   _____[Name]

_____ Father   [Age]_____   _____[Name]

_____ Children   [Age(s)]_____   _____[Name(s)]

This evaluation is: _____ Court-ordered

_____ Joint parental request

Requested by: _____

The evaluation may include interviews with all parties, review of records, collateral interviews, testing, and telephone contacts.

_____[Examiner]_____ will be immune from sanctions or civil litigation.

_____   _____
[Mother]   [Date]   [Guardian Ad-Litem]   [Date]

_____   _____
[Father]   [Date]   [Other]   [Date]

Date: _____

Witness: _____

4.20

Form 15a   Informed Consent—Child Custody/Visitation Evaluation

Parents' Names: (Mother) _Jane Doe_

(Father) _Albert Doe_

(Others) _____

Children: _Stephanie_   Age: _7_

Mark   Age: _9_

_____   Age: _____

_____   Age: _____

Domiciliary Status: _Currently both children reside with mother. 72-hour visitation at father's apartment on alternate weekends. Six weeks with father during summer._

Legal Status: _Shared parental responsibility. Mother is primary custodian. Father seeks extended visitation._

Permission is granted to ___Dr. R. Roe___ to conduct a psychological evaluation of:

_X_	Mother	_42_	_Jane_
_X_	Father	_44_	_Albert_
_X_	Children	_7 & 9_	_Stephanie & Mark_

This evaluation is: _X_   Court-ordered

_____   Joint parental request

Requested by: _Judge Robert Gates_

The evaluation may include interviews with all parties, review of records, collateral interviews, testing, and telephone contacts.

_____Dr. Roe_____ will be immune from sanctions or civil litigation.

_____   _____
[Mother]   [Date]   [Guardian Ad-Litem]   [Date]

_____   _____
[Father]   [Date]   [Other]   [Date]

Date: _____

Witness: _____

4.21

Form 16 Informed Consent—Custody and Visitation Evaluation

I understand that I will be participating in a custody and visitation evaluation involving
_____ .
[Name]

During the course of this evaluation, I understand that I will be interviewed, I will be given psychological tests, and these procedures will be subjected to a standard psychological analysis. A report will be written of my psychological evaluation. Together with psychological evaluations of all of the parties noted above, this will be part of a comprehensive custody and visitation evaluation that will consider each parent's assets, liabilities, and opportunities to improve their ability to meet the best interests of the children.

I understand that all aspects of this evaluation will be made available to both parents. I give my permission for my portion of the assessment and that of the children to be so-included.

_____
[Signature]

_____

_____
[Witnessed]

_____
[Date]

Form 16a Informed Consent—Custody and Visitation Evaluation

I understand that I will be participating in a custody and visitation evaluation involving
Mr. Jones, Mrs. Smith (re: Jones), Sammy and Richard Jones and myself .

During the course of this evaluation, I understand that I will be interviewed, I will be given psychological tests, and these procedures will be subjected to a standard psychological analysis. A report will be written of my psychological evaluation. Together with psychological evaluations of all of the parties noted above, this will be part of a comprehensive custody and visitation evaluation that will consider each parent's assets, liabilities, and opportunities to improve their ability to meet the best interests of the children.

I understand that all aspects of this evaluation will be made available to both parents. I give my permission for my portion of the assessment and that of the children to be so-included.

_____
[Signature]

_____
Walter R. Smith
[Stepfather]

_____
[Witnessed]

_____
_4-18-98_
[Date]

Form 17   Informed Consent—Release of Records

You have been referred to be examined psychologically. A report will be made on the basis of this examination to the referring attorney(s):

_____

_____

Your examination will consist of a series of standardized psychological tests and interviews. The results, and any material associated with the results will be directed to the above-named person(s).

Any questions that may arise as to the results of the examination must be directed to the referring attorney or to your own attorney.

Permission is hereby given to ____[Examiner]_____ to release clinical information and/or test results about: _____[Examinee]_____

Date: _____

Signed: _____

Relationship: _____

Witness: _____

Form 18   Informed Consent

Date: _____

I, _____ [Examinee] _____
agree to interviews and psychological tests to be given to me by _____ [Examiner] _____
who has explained to me that these interviews and psychological tests have been requested by
_____.

_____ [Examiner] _____ has further explained to me in detail that the purpose of these
psychological tests is to prepare a written psychological report concerning _____
_____.

_____ [Examiner] _____ has further informed me that this work will be confidential and
privileged except for _____.
No other reports will be made except by my specific permission or by appropraite court order.

Signature: _____

Witnessed: _____

Form 19   Authorization for Release of Psychological Information

Regarding: _____   DOB: _____

To: _____[Examiner]_____

I, _____, hereby consent and authorize you to release specified information concerning the above named individual to:

_____

_____

_____

The information shall include: _____

_____

I understand that I may revoke this consent at any time except to the extent that action based on this consent has already been taken. This informed consent for the release of information will automatically expire without further action ninety days after the date on which it was signed.

I hereby release _____[Examiner]_____ from all legal responsibility that may arise from the release of the above requested information. This authorization is fully understood and it is made voluntarily and with informed consent on my part.

_____   _____
          [Signature]   [Witness]

_____   _____
    [Signature of parent/guardian]   [Date]

_____   _____
            [Date]

4.26

Form 20   Permission to Release Confidential Records

It is requested that you read and sign this Permission to Release Confidential Records. These records have been requested by:

_____

You will be given a series of standard psychological tests and interviews. The results of these and the materials themselves may be released to the above person or agency. Reports and summaries can also be released.

Permission is hereby given to _____[Examiner]_____ to release clinical information and/or test results to:

_____

About: _____

Date: _____

Signed: _____

Relationship: _____

Form 21　Permission to Release Confidential Records

To: _____

_____

_____

Re: _____

Permission is hereby given to release clinical information about the above-named person to:

_____.

Signed: _____

Date: _____　　Relationship: _____

Form 22   Family History—Child

Date: _____ Informant: _____ By: _____

	Mother (M)	Father (F)

Name:

Age:

Occupation:

Education:

Health:

Personal Style:

Siblings: Additional Notes:

Others:

Socioeconomic level:

Climate: Interaction of Mother (M)

Observations: Interaction of Father (F)

Mother:

Father:

DOB: Age:

Pre & Post Natal: **Grandparents:**

Birth:

Feed:

TT:

1st year:

2–5th year:

Medical: **Religion:**

Physician:

T&A:

Other:

U.C.D.:

Immunizations:

Reg. Compl.:

Pub.:

Sex Ed.:

Additional:

Unconc:

Fever:

Seizures:

During 1st 8 Years: **Trauma:**

Dizziness:

Headaches:

Poor Sleep:

Sinistrality in Family:

School: _____ Performance Below Potential

Friends: _____ Socially Embarrassing

Home: **Homework:**

Room:

Recr:

Sibs:

Meals:

Discipline:

Camp:

Sports:

Hobbies:

Dating:

Allowance:

Bedtime:

Chores:

4.30

Personal Adjustment

Age:	0	1	2	3	4	5	6	7	8	9	10	11	12	13	14
	:	:	:	:	:	:	:	:	:	:	:	:	:	:	:
Nail biting	0	0	0	0	0	0	0	0	0	0	0	0	0	0	0
Crying	0	0	0	0	0	0	0	0	0	0	0	0	0	0	0
Thumbsucking	0	0	0	0	0	0	0	0	0	0	0	0	0	0	0
Enuresis	0	0	0	0	0	0	0	0	0	0	0	0	0	0	0
Soiling	0	0	0	0	0	0	0	0	0	0	0	0	0	0	0
Somnabulism	0	0	0	0	0	0	0	0	0	0	0	0	0	0	0
Vomiting	0	0	0	0	0	0	0	0	0	0	0	0	0	0	0
Stuttering	0	0	0	0	0	0	0	0	0	0	0	0	0	0	0
Masturbation	0	0	0	0	0	0	0	0	0	0	0	0	0	0	0
Nightmares	0	0	0	0	0	0	0	0	0	0	0	0	0	0	0
Night terrors	0	0	0	0	0	0	0	0	0	0	0	0	0	0	0
Fearful	0	0	0	0	0	0	0	0	0	0	0	0	0	0	0
Cruelty	0	0	0	0	0	0	0	0	0	0	0	0	0	0	0
Tantrums	0	0	0	0	0	0	0	0	0	0	0	0	0	0	0
Destructiveness	0	0	0	0	0	0	0	0	0	0	0	0	0	0	0
Quarrelsome	0	0	0	0	0	0	0	0	0	0	0	0	0	0	0
Jealous	0	0	0	0	0	0	0	0	0	0	0	0	0	0	0
Uncooperative	0	0	0	0	0	0	0	0	0	0	0	0	0	0	0
Excess energy	0	0	0	0	0	0	0	0	0	0	0	0	0	0	0
Lying	0	0	0	0	0	0	0	0	0	0	0	0	0	0	0
Stealing	0	0	0	0	0	0	0	0	0	0	0	0	0	0	0
Shyness	0	0	0	0	0	0	0	0	0	0	0	0	0	0	0
Dependency	0	0	0	0	0	0	0	0	0	0	0	0	0	0	0
Lacks self-confidence	0	0	0	0	0	0	0	0	0	0	0	0	0	0	0
Sensitiveness	0	0	0	0	0	0	0	0	0	0	0	0	0	0	0
Mood swings	0	0	0	0	0	0	0	0	0	0	0	0	0	0	0

Date: _9-20-98_   Informant: _Mother, Father, Stepmother, Stepfather_   By: _THB_

	Mother (M)	Stepmother	Stepfather	Father (F)
Name:	Jane	Mary	Bill	Jack
Age:	32	31	29	38
Occupation:	Executive Secretary	Correctional Officer	Insurance	Detective—P.D.
Education:	H.S.	H.S.+	14	14 (A.A.)
Health:	Good	OK	Good	Fine
Personal Style:	Likes good behavior. Fair. Corrects constr.	Short-tempered, but honest	Easygoing	Stern

Siblings: Bill Jr. 10 mo. loves him, no problems

Additional Notes:

Custody, shared
P. caretaker—mother
Visitation—liberal
No conflicts
Negotiated holidays and vacations

Others: Stepgrandparents—good
P. Grandparents—good
Mother's aunt and cousins—good

Socioeconomic level: Father 39K 3 BR apt.
Mother 55K 4 BR Home

Climate: Father   Pretty organized
Mother   Same

Interaction of Mother (M)

Firm but available
Stepmother watchful & critical

Observations:

Mother:	Somewhat stiff, wants to help
Father:	Traditional, dominant, flexible
Stepmother:	Easily annoyed
Stepfather:	Pleasant, passive

Interaction of Father (F)

We have a good time
We play & laugh a lot
Stepfather watch T.V., help with homework

DOB: _7-22-91_ Age: 7-2

Pre & Post Natal:

Birth: 8'4" 1st No difficulty—Mother or child
Feed: Bottle—cup? 9 mo. No problems
TT: 1–1 1/2 years. OK
1st year: OK
2–5th Year: Normal

Grandparents:

Stepgrandparents:
Local, good relationship
Paternal grandparents:
Not as frequent but good

Medical:
Physician: *Wm. Jason, M.D., Winston, FL*
T&A: *N*
Other: *Broken clavicle age 2. Did OK. Some sinus and nose bleeds.*
U.C.D.: *CP. Bad. Facial scars.*
Immunizations: *Yes*
Reg. Compl.: *Pain in legs, chest. Stopped a year ago.*
Pub.: *No*
Sex Ed.: *No*

Additional:
Unconc: *N*
Fever: *N*
Seizures: *N*

During 1st 8 Years:
Dizziness: *N*
Headaches: *Until 1 year ago. Now infrequent*
Poor Sleep: *N*
Sinistrality in Family: *Not known*

School: *Play school. Had good time & adjust. 1st Willow, "Hyperactive." Poor concentration. 2nd Willow, remains "Hyperactive" D. not complete assign.*

Friends:
Easily
Follower
Sleep over—both @ <u>his</u> homes. Not @ theirs

Home:
Room: *Both homes—own room.*
Enjoys posters
Recr: *Movies, T.V. (1 hr. day school, 2 hrs. weekends)*
Sibs: *OK*
Meals: *Picky eater. Mother concerned re: nutrition*
Discipline: *Father—deprivation. Mother—also. Occasionally spanks when frustrated. Stepparents discipline*
Camp: *Day camp last summer—enjoyed*
Sports: *Soccer, skateboarding*
Hobbies: *Stickers*
Dating: *N*
Allowance: *Tried by mother—irresponsible—stopped*

Bedtime: *8:30 P.M.–6:30 A.M.*
Chores: *Mother home—Keep room clean, make bed, dust & sweep room. Father home—No regular chores. He helps out.*

Religion:
Irregular attend. Both families

Trauma:
None known

Father family—red headedness
Mother family—twins
1st & 2nd
__X__ **Performance Below Potential**

__X__ **Socially Embarrassing**
Touching
Hyperactivity

<u>Homework:</u>
None

Wide range of emotional responses:
Irritable
Impulsive
D. learn from experiences
Stubborn
D. complete projects
D. follow directions
Creates conflict in family
Has good heart
Kind to small animals

Personal Adjustment

		Parents Divorce			(M) remarriage		(F) remarriage	step-brother born			current age					
Age:		**0**	**1**	**2**	**3**	**4**	**5**	**6**	**7**	**8**	**9**	**10**	**11**	**12**	**13**	**14**
		:	:	:	:	:	:	:	:	:	:	:	:	:	:	:
Nail biting	N	0	0	0	0	0	0	0	0	0	0	0	0	0	0	0
Crying	N	0	0	0	0	0	0	0	0	0	0	0	0	0	0	0
Thumbsucking	Y	0	0	0	0	0	0	0	0	0	0	0	0	0	0	0
Enuresis	Y	0	0	0	0	0	0	0	0	0	0	0	0	0	0	0
Soiling	N	0	0	0	0	0	0	0	0	0	0	0	0	0	0	0
Somnabulism	Y	0	0	0	0	0	0	0	0	0	0	0	0	0	0	0
Vomiting	N	0	0	0	0	0	0	0	0	0	0	0	0	0	0	0
Stuttering	N	0	0	0	0	0	0	0	0	0	0	0	0	0	0	0
Masturbation	N	0	0	0	0	0	0	0	0	0	0	0	0	0	0	0
Nightmares	N	0	0	0	0	0	0	0	0	0	0	0	0	0	0	0
Night terrors	N	0	0	0	0	0	0	0	0	0	0	0	0	0	0	0
Fearful	N	0	0	0	0	0	0	0	0	0	0	0	0	0	0	0
Cruelty	N	0	0	0	0	0	0	0	0	0	0	0	0	0	0	0
Tantrums	Y	0	0	0	0	0	0	0	0	0	0	0	0	0	0	0
Destructiveness	Y	0	0	0	0	0	0	0	0	0	0	0	0	0	0	0
Quarrelsome	Y	0	0	0	0	0	0	0	0	0	0	0	0	0	0	0
Jealous	N	0	0	0	0	0	0	0	0	0	0	0	0	0	0	0
Uncooperative	Y	0	0	0	0	0	0	0	0	0	0	0	0	0	0	0
Excess energy	Y	0	0	0	0	0	0	0	0	0	0	0	0	0	0	0
Lying	N	0	0	0	0	0	0	0	0	0	0	0	0	0	0	0
Stealing	N	0	0	0	0	0	0	0	0	0	0	0	0	0	0	0
Shyness	N	0	0	0	0	0	0	0	0	0	0	0	0	0	0	0
Dependency	N	0	0	0	0	0	0	0	0	0	0	0	0	0	0	0
Lack self-confidence	Y	0	0	0	0	0	0	0	0	0	0	0	0	0	0	0
Sensitiveness	Y	0	0	0	0	0	0	0	0	0	0	0	0	0	0	0
Mood swings	N	0	0	0	0	0	0	0	0	0	0	0	0	0	0	0

4.34

Form 23   Adult History

Name: _____ DOB: _____ Age: _____

Needs Assessment

Current Complaints: **Greatest Stress:**

Symptoms:

Goals/Questions:

Born: **Religion:**

Mother:

Father: **Grandparents:**

Siblings:

Others:

Family Conflicts:

Childhood/Adolescence:

Education: **Vocational:**

High School
College
Other
Extracurricular act.

Service:

Criminal Justice System:

Medical: **Neurological:**

Dr.:   Accidents:

Curr.:   Illness:

Ill. & Inj.:   Poison:

Medic.:   Electrical:

Sleep: Unconsciousness:

Eat: Convulsions:

Other:

Subject uses:

_____ Tobacco

_____ Alcohol

_____ Substance

_____ Caffeine

Sexual History:

Early: Menarch:

Education: Climax:

Adolescence: Problems:

Adult: Attitudes:

Marital: Trauma:

   First Year:

   Last Year:

   Extramarital:

Best Friend:

Current:

Casual:

Hobbies:

Social:

Physical:

Marriage:

1st: Age: Children:

            Spouse:

            Circum:

Other:

Current:

Problems: Assets:

Form 23a   Adult History

Name: _Jones, Timothly L._ **DOB:** _1-12-66_ **Age:** _32-4_

Needs Assessment

Current Complaints:

4-14-98. I'm in a bad situation. I don't know what's going on. I don't remember anything. I didn't do what they say I did. How could I do it if I remember nothing.
You might be one of "them."

Greatest Stress:

I shouldn't be in the jail. It's a plot against me. I'm innocent.

Symptoms:

I can't remember anything about the last three years.
There are people talking about me.
Sometimes I feel there are bugs crawling on me.

Goals/Questions:

There's no need for me to be in jail. They are making up a case against me. The lawyer they've assigned to me is part of the scheme. I need a good doctor to fix the brain damage they gave me.

Born:

St. Louis, MO

Mother: 67. Housewife. Depression.

Father: 1992. Cancer.

Siblings: Male—42. UPS driver.
               Female—48. Teacher.

Others:

Religion:

Baptist. Irregular attendance.

Grandparents:

Never knew them.

Family Conflicts:

Parents divorced when subject 12. Neither remarried.
Father drank heavily. 5 years in prison—embezzlement.
Mother frequently depressed.

Childhood/Adolescence:

I can't remember.

Education:

High School   St. Louis
College   1 year—George Mason University
Other   H.R. Block Tax Training
Extracurricular act.   No

Vocational:

Bookkeeper

Service: 6 months U.S. Army. Released "For convenience of the government"

Criminal Justice System:

I can't remember.
They say I stole money. I can't remember anything.
It's some kind of plot. I think my lawyer is in on it.

Medical:

Dr.: *I can't remember*

Curr.: *I'm sick*

Ill. & Inj.: *I fell and hurt my head. I can't remember when.*

Medic.: *Tylenol*

Sleep: *They talk trash to me when I'm trying to sleep*

Eat: *OK*

Other:

Subject uses:

  __Y__   Tobacco *2 packs a day*

  __N__   Alcohol

  __N__   Substance

  __Y__   Caffeine *6 cups of coffee per day*
                     2 colas per day

Neurological:

Accidents: *Yes—Fell. Don't know when*

Illness: *I'm sick now*

Poison: *They may be poisoning my food*

Electrical: *I don't know*

Unconsciousness: *I can't remember*

Convulsions: *I can't remember*

Sexual History:

Early: *I can't remember*

Education: *I can't remember*

Adolescence: *I can't remember*

Adult: *I can't remember*

Marital:

  First Year: *I can't remember*
  Last Year: *I can't remember*
  Extramarital: *I can't remember*

Menarch: *N/A*

Climax:

Problems: *Don't know*

Attitudes: *Don't know*

Trauma: *I can't remember*

Best Friend: *Everyone is against me.*

Current:

Casual: *Read. Try to remember but I can't*

Hobbies: *Trying to remember*

Social: *No*

Physical: *Walk*

Marriage:

1st: Age: *I can't remember*
           Spouse:
           Circum:

Other: *Married again last year. Faye.*

Children: *I can't remember*

Current:

Problems

I'm in jail.

Assets

She's the only one on my side.

Form 24 Test Room Schedule

Name: _____ DOB: _____ Age: _____ Grade: _____

Date Scheduled:				DR.	TR	Date	Day	Hours
History:	____	____	____ ( )	____	____	____	____	____
XIT #1	____	____	____ ( )	____	____	____	____	____
XIT #2	____	____	____ ( )	____	____	____	____	____

Totals: DR. _____ TR _____ Workup _____

Interviews

____ History
____ Interview
____ Interview
____ Interview

____ _____

____ _____

Intelligence/Development

____ AFRPV   _ QT
____ PPVT L/M
____ Wonderlic Personnel Test
____ Binet L M
____ Bayley
____ Cattel
____ KABC
____ Raven PM
____ Minn Develop
____ Vineland Adaptive   ____ Soc Mat
____ Normative Adapt Behavior Checklist (NABC)
____ Comp Behav Rating Scale for Child (CBRSC)
____ WPPSI-R
____ WISC-III
____ WAIS-R ____ WAIS ____ WB ____ WAIS-III

__ Inform	__ Picture Comp
__ Comp	__ Picture Arrang
__ Arithmetic	__ Block Design
__ Similarities	__ Digit Symbol-Coding
__ Digit Span	__ Object Assem
__ Vocabulary	__ Matrix Reasoning
__ Symbol Search	__ Letter-Number Seq.

Aptitude

FACT

____ Insp	____ Assem	____ Arith
____ Cod	____ Scales	____ Patt
____ Mem	____ Coord	____ Compon
____ Prec	____ Judg &	____ Tables
____ Mech	____ Comp	____ Exp

____ Brief Speech Evaluation
____ Brief Hearing

Neuropsychology

____ Reitan Sens Deficit   ____ A   ____ C
____ Category (BK) Test
____ Wechsler MS __ I __ II __ R __ III
____ Wells & Ruesch-AAA
____ MFD—Graham-Kendall
____ Indiana-Reitan Short Form
____ Torque ____ Repeat ____ Parents
____ Hand Dynamometer
____ Lezak -Rey 15 Items
____ LNNB ____ I ____ II ___ Child
____ Neuropsychological Sign/Symptom List
____ Spiral Aftereffects Test
____ Neurobehavioral Cognitive Status
____ FL Kind Screen (Satz)
____ Wisconsin Card Sort
____ Portland Digit Recognition Test
____ Dementia, Alzheimer's Type
____ NST   ____ Trails A&B
____ Symbol Digit Modalities Test (PDRT)
____ Stroop Neuro Screening Test (SNST)
____ Rey Complex Fig Test & Recognition Trial
____ Hiscock Forced Choice Test

Achievement

____ Metro Achievement FM JS

____ Pre-Primer	____ Elementary
____ Primer	____ Intermediate
____ Primary 1	____ Advanced 1
____ Primary 2	____ Advanced 2

____ Gates MacGinitie Reading Readiness
____ Nelson-Denny __ E __ F __ G __ H
____ Gates MacGinitie Reading ____ Prim

____ D	FM	1	2	3
____ E	FM	1	2	3
____ F	Form	1		

____ Stanford Task
____ WRAT
____ HS Essentials
____ Metropolitan Reading ____ I ____ II
____ Mini-Battery of Achievement (MBA)
____ Wonderlic Basic Skills Test (WBST)

4.39

Forensic

____ Georgia Court Competency
____ Harvard Competency Screening Test
____ Rogers CRAS
____ Visitation Plan Questionnaire

Interest

____ Strong Interest Inventory
____ Wrenn Study Habits
____ Voc Guid Sum
____ SD Search
____ SRA Typing Skills
____ Steno Aptitude
____ General Clerical
____ Thurstone Typing

Marital

____ Martial Audit   ____ SRA
____ Martial Audit Inventory
____ Marital Diag   ____ Mar Roles
____ Mar Satisf   ____ MHP
____ Marital Adjustment Inventory

Miscellaneous

____ Clinical Observations
____ Psychosocial Pain Inventory
____ Structured Interview of Reported Symptoms
____ _____
____ _____
____ _____
____ _____
____ _____
____ _____
____ _____
____ _____
____ _____
____ _____
____ _____
____ _____

Personality

____ TAT
__ 1   __ 2   __ 3BM   __ 4
__ 5   __ 6BM   __ 6GF   __ 7BM
__ 7GF   __ 8BM   __ 8GF   __ 9BM
__ 9GF   __ 10   __ 11   __ 12BG
__ 12M   __ 12F   __ 13MF   __ 14
__ 15   __ 16   __ 17BM   __ 17GF
__ 18BM   __ 18GF   __ 19   __ 20
__ Dictation __ Write
____ Rorschach
____ H-T   ____ DAP
____ SC   ____ FSC   ____ TASC   ____ CSC
____ TA?
____ Quality of Life
____ MMPI   ____ MMPI-2   ____ MMPI-A
____ 16PF
____ PAI
____ CPI
____ Millon
____ CAQ
____ ALCADD
____ FIRO-B
____ Edwards Personal Preference Schedule
____ NEO PI
____ Family Draw
____ PIC
____ Child Behavior Profile
____ Mother-Child Rel Eval
____ Parent Stress Index
____ Multidimension Child Pers
____ Holmes Stress Scale (SRE)
____ Parent/Child Relationship Inventory
____ _____
____ _____
____ _____

Form 24a   Test Room Schedule

Name: _Jones, Timothy_		**DOB:** _1-12-66_	**Age:** _32-4_	**Grade:** _13_	

	DR.	**TR**	**Date**	**Day**	**Hours**
Date Scheduled: _3-20-98_					
History: _Tues._ _4-14_ _1998_ (1)	___	_3_	_4-14_	_Tues._	_3_
XIT #1 _Report to Asst._ ( )	_1_	_3_	_4-15_	_Wed._	_4_
U.S. Attorney Cates ( )	_1_	_3_	_4-16_	_Thurs._	_4_
and to Judge. **Totals:**	**DR.** _3_	**TR** _9_		**Workup** ___	

Interviews

X   History _(Dr.)_
X   Interview _(Dr.)_
___   Interview
___   Interview
___ _____
___ _____

Intelligence/Development

___   AFRPV   ___   QT
___   PPVT L/M
___   Wonderlic Personnel Test
___   Binet L M
___   Bayley
___   Cattel
___   KABC
___   Raven PM
___   Minn Develop
___   Vineland Adaptive   ___   Soc Mat
___   Normative Adapt Behavior Checklist (NABC)
___   Comp Behav Rating Scale for Child (CBRSC)
___   WPPSI-R
___   WISC-III
___   WAIS-R ___ WAIS ___ WB X WAIS-III

    X Inform   X Picture Comp
    X Comp   X Picture Arrang
    X Arithmetic   X Block Design
    X Similarities   X Digit Symbol-Coding
    X Digit Span   X Object Assem
    X Vocabulary   ___ Matrix Reasoning
    X Symbol Search   ___ Letter-Number Seq.

Aptitude
FACT

___ Insp	___ Assem	___ Arith
___ Cod	___ Scales	___ Patt
___ Mem	___ Coord	___ Compon
___ Prec	___ Judg &	___ Tables
___ Mech	___ Comp	___ Exp

___   Brief Speech Evaluation
___   Brief Hearing

Neuropsychology

___   Reitan Sens Deficit   ___ A   ___ C
X   Category (BK) Test
___   Wechsler MS ___ I ___ II ___ R X III
___   Wells & Ruesch-AAA
___   MFD—Graham-Kendall
___   Indiana-Reitan Short Form
___   Torque ___ Repeat ___ Parents
___   Hand Dynamometer
X   Lezak -Rey 15 Items
X   LNNB ___ I X II ___ Child
___   Neuropsychological Sign/Symptom List
___   Spiral Aftereffects Test
___   Neurobehavioral Cognitive Status
___   FL Kind Screen (Satz)
X   Wisconsin Card Sort _(Dr.)_
___   Portland Digit Recognition Test
___   Dementia, Alzheimer's Type
___   NST ___ Trails A&B
___   Symbol Digit Modalities Test (PDRT)
___   Stroop Neuro Screening Test (SNST)
___   Rey Complex Fig Test & Recognition Trial
X   Hiscock Forced Choice Test

Achievement

___   Metro Achievement FM JS
    ___ Pre-Primer   ___ Elementary
    ___ Primer   ___ Intermediate
    ___ Primary 1   ___ Advanced 1
    ___ Primary 2   ___ Advanced 2
___   Gates MacGinitie Reading Readiness
X   Nelson-Denny X E ___ F ___ G ___ H
___   Gates MacGinitie Reading ___ Prim

___	D	FM	1	2	3
___	E	FM	1	2	3
___	F	Form	1		

___   Stanford Task
___   WRAT
___   HS Essentials
___   Metropolitan Reading ___ I ___ II
___   Mini-Battery of Achievement (MBA)
___   Wonderlic Basic Skills Test (WBST)

Forensic

____ Georgia Court Competency
_X_ Harvard Competency Screening Test
____ Rogers CRAS
____ Visitation Plan Questionnaire

Interest

____ Strong Interest Inventory
____ Wrenn Study Habits
____ Voc Guid Sum
____ SD Search
____ SRA Typing Skills
____ Steno Aptitude
____ General Clerical
____ Thurstone Typing

Marital

____ Martial Audit   ____ SRA
____ Martial Audit Inventory
____ Marital Diag   ____ Mar Roles
____ Mar Satisf   ____ MHP
____ Marital Adjustment Inventory

Miscellaneous

_X_ Clinical Observations _(Dr.)_
____ Psychosocial Pain Inventory
_X_ Structured Interview of Reported Symptoms
     _(Dr.)_

____ _____
____ _____
____ _____
____ _____
____ _____
____ _____
____ _____
____ _____
____ _____
____ _____

Personality

____ TAT

__ 1   __ 2   __ 3BM   __ 4
__ 5   __ 6BM   __ 6GF   __ 7BM
__ 7GF   __ 8BM   __ 8GF   __ 9BM
__ 9GF   __ 10   __ 11   __ 12BG
__ 12M   __ 12F   __ 13MF   __ 14
__ 15   __ 16   __ 17BM   __ 17GF
__ 18BM   __ 18GF   __ 19   __ 20
__ Dictation __ Write

_X_ Rorschach _(Dr.)_
____ H-T   _X_ DAP
____ SC   ____ FSC   ____ TASC   ____ CSC
____ TA?
____ Quality of Life
____ MMPI _X_ MMPI-2   ____ MMPI-A
_X_ 16PF
____ PAI
____ CPI
____ Millon
____ CAQ
____ ALCADD
____ FIRO-B
____ Edwards Personal Preference Schedule

____ NEO PI
____ Family Draw
____ PIC
____ Child Behavior Profile
____ Mother-Child Rel Eval
____ Parent Stress Index
____ Multidimension Child Pers
____ Holmes Stress Scale (SRE)
____ Parent/Child Relationship Inventory

____ _____
____ _____
____ _____

Form 25 Family Conference

Name: _____ Date: _____ Phone: _____

In Person: _____

Age: _____   Grade: _____

Participants:

_____ Mother   _____ Other: _____

_____ Father

_____ Sibs

Purpose:

Discussion:

Interpretation/Recommendations:

Form 25a   Family Conference

Name: _Jones, Tommy_ _____ Date: _2-19-98_   Phone: _____

In Person: ___X___

Age: __15-6__   Grade: __9.6__

Participants:

__X__ Mother   _____ Other: _(Uncle) Charles Jones_ _____

__X__ Father

_____ Sibs

Purpose:

   1. To obtain family's observations about Tommy since the motor vehicle accident of 2-11-97.

Discussion:

   1. Family agrees that the most significant changes in Tommy include:
      a. Pain in legs and back.
      b. Immediate memory problems.
      c. Irritability.
      d. Social withdrawal.
      e. Fatigue.
      f. Dizziness.
      g. Disrupted sleep.
      h. Loss of "sense of humor."
   2. Family was interviewed for The Neuropsychological Symptom/Sign/Course Form.

Interpretation/Recommendations:

Name: _____ DOB: _____ Age: _____ Date: _____

Education: _____

Date of Trauma/Illness: _____ Incident: _____

A. Event:

_____ Unconscious. Time: _____

_____ Anterograde Amnesia. Time: _____

_____ Retrograde Amnesia. Time: _____

_____ Speech Anomalies: _____

_____

_____ Visual Anomalies: _____

_____

_____ Motor Anomalies: _____

_____

_____ Cognitive Anomalies: _____

_____

Other signs or symptoms at time of trauma or illness:

Immediate Course (90 Days):

Medical Procedures:

_____ Neurologic: _____   _____ CT Scans _____

_____ Skull X-Rays: _____   _____ EEG _____

_____ Other: _____

B. Changes Since Accident or Incident (Approximate time after Event _____)

Had   + Still Have   0–Observed

1.   Communication

_____ Expressive Speech _____

_____ Hearing _____

_____ Writing _____

2.   Sensory & Motor

_____ Dizziness _____

_____ Nausea _____

_____ Pain _____

_____ Noise/Light _____

_____ Fine Motor _____

_____ Gross Motor _____

_____ Numbness _____

_____ Body-In-Space _____

_____ Headaches _____

_____ Insomnia _____

_____ Convulsions _____

_____ Bleeding _____

_____ Sleep Problems _____

_____ Fatigue _____

3.   Visual

_____ Diplopia or Blurring _____

_____ Other Changes _____

4.   Cognition & Mentation

_____ Concentration Difficulty _____

_____ Confusion _____

_____ Decreased Initiative _____

_____ Increased Rigidity _____

_____ Memory Loss _____

Recent _____

Past _____

_____ Difficulty Organizing _____

_____ Concrete Thinking _____

_____ Disorientation _____

_____ Sluggish Ideation _____

_____ Increased Dependency _____

_____ Impaired Judgment _____

5.   Emotion

_____ Agitation _____

_____ Depression _____

_____ Anxiety _____

_____ Impatience _____

_____ Paranoid Thinking _____

_____ Sexual Problems _____

_____ Social Difficulties _____

_____ Irritability & Complaints _____

_____ Tantrums _____

C. Addenda

6.   Factitious

_____ Change in glove or shoe size

_____ Sudden brittleness of nails

_____ Sudden change in hair thickness

_____ Allergic reaction to gold jewelry

_____ Increased/decreased scalp oiliness

_____ Sweating behind ears

_____ Increased colds or sore throats

1. Informant: _____

2. By: _____

Form 26a Neuropsychological Symptom/Sign/Course

Name: _Jones, Tommy_____ DOB: _6-4-82_ Age: _15-6_ Date: _2-19-98_
Education: _9.6_

Date of Trauma/Illness: _2-11-97_____ Incident: _Automobile accident_____

A. Event:

Yes Unconscious. Time: _2:15 P.M.—Noon next day_____
Yes Anterograde Amnesia. Time: _13 hours_____
Yes Retrograde Amnesia. Time: _3 hours_____
_?_ Speech Anomalies: _____

_?_ Visual Anomalies: _____
_____

Yes Motor Anomalies: _____
_____

Yes Cognitive Anomalies: _____
_____

Other signs or symptoms at time of trauma or
illness:
Glasgow Coma Scale—8

Immediate Course (90 Days):
Hospital 10 days
Rehab. 14 days (Hospital)

Medical Procedures:
Yes Neurologic: _Abn (see reports)_____   _Yes_ CT Scans _Abn (see reports)_____
Yes Skull X-Rays: _Abn (see reports)_____   _No_ EEG _____
_____ Other: _____

B. Changes Since Accident or Incident (Approximate time after Event _____)

✓ Had   + Still Have   0–Observed

1. **Communication**
   _+_ Expressive Speech _Blocks_____
   ____ Hearing _____
   _+_ Writing _Hard to decipher_____
2. **Sensory & Motor**
   _✓_ Dizziness _____
   _✓_ Nausea _____
   _+_ Pain _Legs, back_____
   _+_ Noise/Light _Bothered by car lights_____
   _+_ Fine Motor _Drops things_____
   ____ Gross Motor _____
   _+_ Numbness _Legs_____
   _+_ Body-In-Space _Bumps into doorways_____
   _+_ Headaches _Daily_____
   _+_ Insomnia _Hard to get to sleep_____
   ____ Convulsions _____
   ____ Bleeding _____
   _+_ Sleep Problems _Wakeful_____
   _+_ Fatigue _____
3. **Visual**
   _✓_ Diplopia or Blurring _First month_____
   ____ Other Changes _____

4. **Cognition & Mentation**
   _+_ Concentration Difficulty _____
   ____ Confusion _____
   _+_ Decreased Initiative _____
   ____ Increased Rigidity _____
   _+_ Memory Loss _____
        Recent _+_ _____
        Past _____
   _+_ Difficulty Organizing _____
   ____ Concrete Thinking _____
   ____ Disorientation _____
   _+_ Sluggish Ideation _____
   _+_ Increased Dependency _____
   ____ Impaired Judgment _____
5. **Emotion**
   _+_ Agitation _____
   _+_ Depression _____
   _+_ Anxiety _____
   _+_ Impatience _____
   _✓_ Paranoid Thinking _____
   ____ Sexual Problems _____
   _+_ Social Difficulties _____
   _+_ Irritability & Complaints _____
   _✓_ Tantrums _For about 2 months_____

C. Addenda

The school took him out of
the gifted program.

6. **Factitious**
   _No_ Change in glove or shoe size
   _No_ Sudden brittleness of nails
   _No_ Sudden change in hair thickness
   _No_ Allergic reaction to gold jewelry

_No_ Increased/decreased scalp oiliness
_No_ Sweating behind ears
_No_ Increased colds or sore throats

1. Informant: _Mother, Father, Uncle Charlie_____
2. By: _Dr. Jones_____

Form 27   Posttraumatic Stress Disorder

Checklist

Name: _____ **Date:** _____ **Trauma Date:** _____

A.   <u>Incident:</u>   _____

_____

_____ 1.   Event involving actual or threatened death or serious injury to self or others.

_____ 2.   Intense fear, helplessness or horror.

B.   <u>Re-Experienced</u>

_____ 1.   Distressing, recurrent, intrusive recollection.

_____ 2.   Recurrent distressing dreams of events.

_____ 3.   Sudden re-living of the event (flashback).

_____ 4.   Intense distress at exposure to cues or events symbolizing event.

_____ 5.   Physiological reactivity when at a place or event symbolizing or resembling the trauma.

C.   <u>Avoidance of Stimuli Associated with the Trauma or Numbing</u>

_____ 1.   Avoids thoughts or feelings associated with the event.

_____ 2.   Avoids activities or situations that arouse recollects of the trauma.

_____ 3.   Inability to recall important aspects of the trauma.

_____ 4.   Markedly diminished interest in significant activities.

_____ 5.   Feelings of detachment or estrangement from other people.

_____ 6.   Restricted range of emotion.

_____ 7.   Sense of foreshortened future and expectations.

D.   <u>Increased Arousal</u>

_____ 1.   Difficulty falling or staying asleep.

_____ 2.   Irritability or outbursts of anger.

_____ 3.   Difficulty concentrating.

_____ 4.   Hypervigilance.

_____ 5.   Startle response.

E.   _____ <u>Duration of Symptoms More Than 1 Month</u>

F.   _____ <u>Clinically Significant Distress or Impairment</u>

4.47

Interview

Expand on the information obtained in the checklist.

B. Event Re-Experienced

1. Distressing, Recurrent, Intrusive Recollection: _____
    _____
    _____
    _____

2. Recurrent, Distressing Dreams of Events: _____
    _____
    _____
    _____

3. Sudden Re-Living of the Event (Flashback): _____
    _____
    _____
    _____

4. Intense Distress at Exposure to Events Symbolizing Event: _____
    _____
    _____
    _____

5. Physiological Reactivity When at a Place or Event Symbolizing or Resembling the Trauma:
    _____
    _____
    _____

C. Avoidance of Stimuli Associated with the Trauma or Numbing

1. Avoids Thoughts or Feelings Associated with the Event: _____
    _____
    _____
    _____

2. Avoid Activities or Situations That Arouse Recollections of the Trauma: _____
    _____
    _____
    _____

3. Inability to Recall Relevant Aspects of the Trauma: _____
    _____
    _____
    _____

4. Markedly Diminished Interest in Significant Activities: _____
_____
_____
_____
_____

5. Feelings of Detachment or Estrangement from Other People: _____
_____
_____
_____
_____

6. Restricted Range of Emotion: _____
_____
_____
_____
_____

7. Sense of Foreshortened Future and Expectations: _____
_____
_____
_____
_____

D. Increased Arousal

1. Difficulty Falling or Staying Asleep: _____
_____
_____
_____
_____

2. Irritability or Outbursts of Anger: _____
_____
_____
_____
_____

3. Difficulty Concentrating: _____
_____
_____
_____
_____

4. Hypervigilance: _____
_____
_____
_____
_____

5. Startle Response: _____
_____
_____
_____
_____

Form 28　Drug Use History

Name: _____

DOB: _____　　　Age: _____　　　Date: _____

Drug	Age of First Use	Age of Last Use	Peak Daily Habit ($)	Daily, Weekly, Sporadic Use and Details
Alcohol				
Amphetamines				
Caffeine				
Cannabis				
Cocaine				
Hallucinogens (LSD)				
Inhalants (Glue)				
Nicotine				
Opioids (Heroin)				
Phencyclidine (PCP)				
Sedatives (Hypnotic or Anxiolytic)				
Barbiturates				
Prescription Drugs				

Form 28a Drug Use History

Name: _Teagarten, Jack_

DOB: ____5-1-60____   Age: __38__   Date: ___4-17-98___

Drug		Age of First Use	Age of Last Use	Peak Daily Habit ($)	Daily, Weekly, Sporadic Use and Details
Alcohol	Yes	14	37		Regularly until arrest last year
Amphetamines	Yes	19	23		To "up" from "Horse" (Heroin)
Caffeine					
Cannabis	Yes	14	23 or 4		Regularly
Cocaine	Yes	25	37		Regularly until arrest last year
Hallucinogens (LSD)	No				
Inhalants (Glue)	No				
Nicotine					
Opioids (Heroin)	Yes	19	23		Regularly until I started with cocaine
Phencyclidine (PCP)	No				
Sedatives (Hypnotic or Anxiolytic)					
Barbiturates	No				
Prescription Drugs					
Percodan		30	37		On and off

Form 29   Medications

Name: _____   Date: _____

Source: Patient: _____   Family: _____   Physician: _____   Record: _____   Containers: _____

Medication	Dosage	Physician	Purpose

Other Notations:

Form 30   Clinical Observations

Patient's Name: _____   Date: _____   By: _____

Time: _____

Initial Observation of Appearance & Test Behavior:

☐ Glasses

☐ Other:

Speech:

Hearing:

Motor:

Socialization:

Cooperation:

Confidence:

Other:

Form 30a   Clinical Observations

Patient's Name: _George Huckle_   Date: ___6-5-98___   By: _THB_____

Time: _4 hrs. 20 min._

Initial Observation of Appearance & Test Behavior:

- Accompanied by wife
- 6'1", 160 lbs
- Brown hair—balding on top
- Blue eyes
- Appears tired or "spacey"

☒ Glasses *for reading*

☒ Other:

  Moustache

Speech:

- Soft.
- Regionally southern.
- Responds simply and slowly.
- Occasionally "mutters" to himself.

Hearing:

- Seems to be within normal limits.

Motor:

- Mostly controlled.
- Occasional "twitches" of hands and lower arms.
- Picks at scabs on his arms continually.

Socialization:

- Very limited.
- Never smiles.
- Responds slowly.
- No eye contact.

Cooperation:

- Minimal.
- Many questions must be asked twice or more.

Confidence:

- Hard to determine.

Other:

- Frequent visits to restroom. Spends a long time there.
- Draws "stick" figures on the Draw-A-Person Test.

Form 31   Assessment Time Log

Patient: _____   By: _____

Date	Time In	Out	Total	Function	By

Form 31a   Assessment Time Log

Patient: _Wilson, James_   By: _THB (Dr.)_
                                                                          PAB (Wm)

Date	Time In	Out	Total	Function	By
5-7	9:00 A.M.	9:55	55'	Initial history with subject	THB
	10:00 A.M.	11:00	60'	History and interview with mother	THB
	9:00 A.M.	12:00	180'	Intelligence testing, reading tests	PAB
	11:00 A.M.	11:15	15'	Observe and participate in testing	THB
	1:15 P.M.	4:00	165'	Continue testings Neuropsych & personality	PAB
	3:00 P.M.	3:30	30'	Observe and participate in testing	THB
5-8	9:00 A.M.	9:40	40'	Harvard competency examination	THB
	9:40 A.M.	12:00	140'	Finish personality and other testing	PAB
	10:00 A.M.	10:45	45'	Telephone interview with subject's parole officer	THB

Form 32   Behavioral Symptomatology of Borderline Personality

_____   1. "I don't know" responses hide fragmentation.

_____   2. Lapses in logical thinking.

_____   3. Episodes of language disorganization.

_____   4. Slippages in reasoning.

_____   5. Idiosyncratic language usage.

_____   6. Fluid, stream of ideas similar to free association.

_____   7. Logical connections between ideas loosened.

_____   8. Reality first perceived accurately then entwined with fantasy or bizarre notions.

_____   9. Overreacts, underreacts, or moves back and forth.

_____   10. Rapid shifts in lability. (Anger—childlike dependency.)

_____   11. Maintains rigid control then suddenly collapses in a flood of emotion.

_____   12. Sexual, dependency, and aggressive feelings appear childlike.

_____   13. Direct gratification almost irresistible.

_____   14. Patchwork of defenses.

_____   15. Regression and intellectualization alternate.

_____   16. Attempts to reduce tension are frantic.

_____   17. Gross denial of obvious realities.

_____   18. Projection.

_____   19. Threats of violence.

_____   20. *Splitting.* (Fluctuation rapidly between grossly inaccurate perceptions of self and others with shifting emotions and contradictory ideas.)

_____   21. Adherence to conventional values and rules falters.

Blau, T. (1988). *Psychotherapy Tradecraft.* New York: Brunner/Mazel.

Kernberg, O. (1975). *Borderline Conditions and Pathological Narcissism.* New York: Aronson.

Knight, R. (1953). Borderline states. *Bulletin of the Menninger Clinic, 17*(1), 1–12.

Wilson, A. (1985). Boundary disturbance in borderline and psychotic states. *Journal of Personality Assessment, 49*(4), 346–355.

Form 33　Glasgow Coma Scale and Trauma Score

Eyes	Open Eyes	4
	Open Eyes on Request	3
	Open Eyes on Pain	2
	Fails to Open Eyes	1
Verbal Response	Appropriate Conversation Oriented to Month and Year	5
	Confused and/or Disoriented	4
	Inappropriate Conversation	3
	Incomprehensible Sounds	2
	No Sounds	1
Motor Response	Follow Simple Directions	6
	Removes Pain Source	5
	Withdraws from Pain Source	4
	Nonpurposeful Flexion (decorticate)	3
	Nonpurposeful Extension (decerebrate)	2
	No Motor Response	1
Apply this score to GCS portion of Trauma Score below:*	Total	

Trauma Score

Respiratory Rate	10–24/min.	4
	25–35/min.	3
	36/min. or greater	2
	1–9/min.	1
	None	0
Respiratory	Normal	1
	Retractive	0
Systolic Blood Pressure	90 mm Hg or greater	4
	70–89 mm Hg	3
	50–69 mm Hg	2
	0–49 mm Hg	1
	No Pulse	0
Capillary Refill	Normal	2
	Delayed	1
	None	0
*Total Glasgow Coma Scale Points	14–15 =	5
	11–13 =	4
	8–10 =	3
	5–7 =	2
	3–4 =	1
Total Trauma Score		1–16

4.58

Form 34   Items Frequently Used to Assess Mental Status in Dementing Patients

Orientation

    Time (year, season, date, day, month)

    Place ("Where are we?," city, town, hospital, ward)

    Person

Concentration and Attention

    Serial sevens (count back from 100 in 7s)

    Counting from 1 to 20

    Counting from 20 to 1

    Months of the year backward

Memory

    Memory span, repetition of digits (digit span)

    Learn names of three objects (number of trials)

    Delayed recall of same three objects (5-minute delay)

Remote Memory

    Date of birth, place of birth, schools attended, occupation

    Names of siblings, wife, and children

    Names of employers

    Name of mayor, president, date of World War II

    Knowledge of current events

Abstract Thinking

    Explain proverbs (e.g., "Don't cry over spilled milk.")

    Similarities (e.g., lion–tiger)

Language

    Name common objects (pen, book, coin)

    Repeat a complex sentence

    Follow a three-stage command

Apraxia

    Copy a geometric design

Form 35   Competency Evaluation Instrument

Name: _____   Date: _____

1. *Appreciation of the charges or allegations.* Assessment of the accused's understanding or literal knowledge of the charges or allegations. It is important that he *understands* of what he is being accused, the consequences of which may be detrimental to him.

   _____ Unacceptable   _____ Questionable   _____ Acceptable   _____ Not Applicable

2. *Appreciation of the range and nature of possible penalties, if applicable, which may be imposed in the proceedings against him.* Assessment of the accused's concrete understanding and appreciation of the conditions and restrictions which could be imposed on him and how long these may endure.

   _____ Unacceptable   _____ Questionable   _____ Acceptable   _____ Not Applicable

3. *Understanding of the adversary nature of the legal process.* Does the accused understand that (a) the responsibility of his attorney is to assist him, (b) the State Attorney's responsibility is to prove his guilt, (c) the Judge is impartial and protects his rights as well as those of the state, and (d) the jury is impartial.

   _____ Unacceptable   _____ Questionable   _____ Acceptable   _____ Not Applicable

4. *Capacity to disclose to his attorney facts pertinent to the proceedings at issue.* Assessment of the accused's capacity to give a consistent, rational, and relevant account of the facts surrounding his alleged offense or the accusations against him. Intelligence, perceptual capacity, memory, and validity of any claimed amnesia should be assessed. Consideration should be given to potential disparity between what he may disclose to a clinician and what he may share with his attorney.

   _____ Unacceptable   _____ Questionable   _____ Acceptable   _____ Not Applicable

5. *Ability to manifest appropriate courtroom behavior.* Assessment of his current behavior and probable behavior when exposed to the stress of courtroom proceedings. Evaluate his beliefs and attitude toward the judicial system.

   _____ Unacceptable   _____ Questionable   _____ Acceptable   _____ Not Applicable

6. *Capacity to testify relevantly.* Assessment of the accused's ability to testify with coherence, relevance, and independence of judgment including both cognitive and affective factors that may impact his ability to communicate.

   _____ Unacceptable   _____ Questionable   _____ Acceptable   _____ Not Applicable

Conclusions:

Evaluator _____

Form 36   Insanity Defense Evaluation

Case Style: _____   **Date Referred:** _____

Records Review:

___ Police reports   ___ Defendant's school records   ___ Pre-event mental health records

___ EMS/Autopsy   ___ Defendant's military records   ___ Post-event mental health records

___ Defendant's post-event statements   ___ Collateral witness statements

___ Pre-event collateral informant interviews   ___ Incarceration records

Legal Records Review:

___ Appropriate state/federal statutes   ___ Affidavits and motions

___ Indictment

Evaluation:

___ Interview(s)   ___ Observation   ___ Intellectual factors

___ Cognitive factors   ___ Reading level   ___ Personality factors

___ Validity evaluations   ___ Check all scoring   ___ Recheck all scoring

___ Time and administration/scoring initials on each test and record

Report:

___ Oral report to judge/retaining attorney   ___ Written report—rough

___ Check all reported scores and percentiles   ___ Cite appropriate references to support opinion

Form 37   Reporting Sanity and Competence Findings

Assuming that the psychologist wishes to avoid answering the ultimate question, results of examinations for sanity and competence might be concluded in the following terms:

Sanity Issues

The review of records and the psychological assessment findings indicate that
Mr. _____ suffers (has suffered or does not suffer or has not suffered) a
mental (and/or neuropsychological) disorder which can result in episodes of confusion, unawareness
and/or distortion of reality. During such episodes it is unlikely that Mr. _____
is aware of or understand the rightness or wrongness of his acts. (During the active phases of this
disorder, Mr. _____ may not be able to control his own behavior).

Competency

Psychological examination of Mr. _____ indicates that he understands the
nature of the charges against him, and what may accrue in the event that he is convicted of such
charges. The psychological examination indicates that Mr. _____ understands
the nature of the relationship that he has with his attorney, and is capable of cooperating in his own
defense. Further, the psychological evaluation indicates that Mr. _____
is capable of making a reasonable appearance during a trial, and acting in his own best interests. He
understands the nature of the trial process, and the role of the judge, the jury, and the various attorneys.

Form 38 Institutional Cost Survey

Institution: Date of Evaluation:

Approximate Annual Fee: $

Services: (X—included, 0 additional fee)

_____   Educational   Other Facilities

_____   Tutorial   _____   _____

_____   Remedial   _____   _____

_____   Psychotherapy   _____   _____

_____   Medical   _____   _____

_____   Social Training   _____   _____

_____   Behavioral Management   _____   _____

_____   Evaluation   _____   _____

_____   Summer Camp   _____   _____

Orientation:

Accreditation:

Other:

Form 38a   Institutional Cost Survey

Institution: *Wilson Orthogenic School*
                      475 Oakland View
                      Sempers, Illiana, 46307

Date of Evaluation: *5-14-98*

Approximate Annual Fee: *$42,000*

Services: (X—included, 0 additional fee)

_X_   Educational

_0_   Tutorial

_X_   Remedial

_0_   Psychotherapy

_X_   Medical

_X_   Social Training

_X_   Behavioral Management

_X_   Evaluation

_0_   Summer Camp

Other Facilities

_X_   *Religious activities*

_X_   *Structured Phys. Ed.*

_X_   *Dance*

_X_   *Aerobics*

_____   _____

_____   _____

_____   _____

_____   _____

Orientation: *Modern; Behavioral Management*

Accreditation: *Midwestern Special Education Secondary School Association*

Other:
1. Very good reports from parents whose children have attended.
2. Recommend sending for catalog and detailed application forms.

Form 39   Clinical Procedures Note

In order to ensure that all clients and patients know the limits of confidentiality and privilege, when an individual first makes an appearance for services (other than forensic), after the introductions are made and before the problem is discussed, the psychologist should give a copy of this statement to the client while presenting it verbally:

Everything we talk about is both confidential and privileged, which means it cannot be discussed outside of this office. Nothing that you say may be used in a legal action. There are exclusions. Every professional person in [State] is legally bound to report to the police or the Child Abuse Registry [Phone Number] any evidence of child abuse that is admitted during their professional contacts or is even reasonably suspected.

Second, anyone who expresses a serious intent to harm themselves or others places upon the psychologist a "duty to warn" by law.

In the event that anyone in a confidential relationship includes an issue of their mental health in any criminal or civil action, the patient's protection of confidentiality and privilege is cancelled.

Have the client sign a copy of the statement indicating that he or she has read/heard it.

Form 40 Limits of Confidentiality

In the course of professional relationships, the psychologist may be called upon to discuss information relating to the case or to transfer records. The limits of confidentiality are broadly included in the following principles:

1. No information about the patient will be transferred to anyone else without the expressed permission of the patient. This must be done in writing as well as by verbal arrangement.

2. Where the patient is a minor, every effort will be made to gain the minor's permission first, and then the permission of the guardian or parent.

3. If issues of sexual abuse of the patient emerge, it is the psychologist's responsibility to convince the patient to report this in the appropriate manner specified by state statute, or, in the event that the patient refuses this permission, to make the report over the patient's objection.

4. It is possible that at future times, various organizations (the state Bar, graduate schools, high-security government agencies and so forth) may request information concerning the services rendered. This information will be forwarded only with the written consent of the patient.

5. No electronic recording of any contacts or interviews will be made without specific written permission from the patient.

_____   _____
[Patient's Name]   [Date]

Form 41   Follow-Up Contacts

Date	Contact (Name, Address, Phone Number)

Form 42   Wechsler Scales—Comparison Sheet

Name: _____   Date: _____   By: _____

	(Date)		(Date)	
	DIQ	**Percentile**	**DIQ**	**Percentile**
Verbal Scales	_____	_____	_____	_____
Performance Scales	_____	_____	_____	_____
Full Scale	_____	_____	_____	_____

Wechsler Subscales
Percentile Rank

Subscale	(Date)	(Date)
Information	_____	_____
Comprehension	_____	_____
Arithmetic	_____	_____
Similarities	_____	_____
(Digit Span)	_____	_____
Vocabulary	_____	_____
Picture Completion	_____	_____
Picture Arrangement	_____	_____
Block Design	_____	_____
Object Assembly	_____	_____
Digit Symbol (Coding)	_____	_____
(Mazes)	_____	_____
(Animal Pegs)	_____	_____
(Symbol Search)	_____	_____

Form 42a   Wechsler Scales—Comparison Sheet

Name: _Doaks, Joseph_   Date: _3-7-98_   By: _DR_

	WAIS (5-17-92)		WAIS-R (2-4-98)	
	DIQ	**Percentile**	**DIQ**	**Percentile**
Verbal Scales	102	55th	81	10th
Performance Scales	94	34th	78	7th
Full Scale	99	47th	79	8th

Wechsler Subscales
Percentile Rank (Age-Related)

Subscale	(5-17-92)	(2-4-98)
Information	63rd	5th
Comprehension	5th	25th
Arithmetic	84th	9th
Similarities	75th	5th
(Digit Span)	37th	25th
Vocabulary	91st	16th
Picture Completion	16th	9th
Picture Arrangement	50th	5th
Block Design	50th	9th
Object Assembly	—	—
Digit Symbol (Coding)	50th	25th
(Mazes)	—	—
(Animal Pegs)	—	—
(Symbol Search)	—	—

Form 43   Wechsler Scales for Children—Comparison Sheet

Name: _____ Date: _____ By: _____

	WISC-R ( )		WISC-III ( )	
	DIQ	Percentile	DIQ	Percentile
Verbal Scales	_____	_____	_____	_____
Performance Scales	_____	_____	_____	_____
Full Scale	_____	_____	_____	_____

Wechsler Subscale Scores
Percentiles

Subscale	WISC-R ( )	WISC-III ( )
Information	_____	_____
Comprehension	_____	_____
Arithmetic	_____	_____
Similarities	_____	_____
(Digit Span)	_____	_____
Vocabulary	_____	_____
Picture Completion	_____	_____
Picture Arrangement	_____	_____
Block Design	_____	_____
Object Assembly	_____	_____
Digit Symbol (Coding)	_____	_____
(Mazes)	_____	_____
(Animal Pegs)	_____	_____
(Symbol Search)	_____	_____

Form 43a   Wechsler Scales for Children—Comparison Sheet

Name: _Farmington, William_ _____ Date: _2-15-98_ By: _DR_ _____

	WISC-R (7-90)		WISC-III (12-97)	
	DIQ	**Percentile**	**DIQ**	**Percentile**
Verbal Scales	133	99th	102	56th
Performance Scales	142	99+th	110	76th
Full Scale	142	99th+	106	66th

Wechsler Subscale Scores
Percentiles

Subscale	WISC-R (7-90)	WISC-III (12-97)
Information	63rd	5th
Comprehension	5th	25th
Arithmetic	84th	9th
Similarities	75th	5th
(Digit Span)	37th	25th
Vocabulary	91st	16th
Picture Completion	16th	9th
Picture Arrangement	50th	5th
Block Design	50th	9th
Object Assembly	—	—
Digit Symbol (Coding)	50th	25th
(Mazes)	—	—
(Animal Pegs)	—	—
(Symbol Search)	—	—

4.71

Form 44   Achievement Tests Comparison Sheet

Name: _____ Date: _____ By: _____

Factor	( ) Percentiles	( ) Percentiles
Reading	_____	_____
Mathematics	_____	_____
Language	_____	_____
Science	_____	_____
Social Studies	_____	_____
Basic Battery	_____	_____
Total Battery	_____	_____

Form 44a   Achievement Tests Comparison Sheet

Name: _Farmington, William_ _____ Date: _2-15-98_   By: _DR_ _____

Factors	(CTBS 7-92) Percentiles	(Metropolitan 12-97) Percentiles
Reading	96th	14th
Mathematics	99th	88th
Language	52nd	38th
Science	99th	54th
Social Studies	68th	35th
Basic Battery	—	—
Total Battery	—	—

Form 45   Testing Comparison Sheet (Up to Three Wechslers)

Name: _____ Date: _____ By: _____

Wechsler

Factor	DIQ	Percentile	DIQ	Percentile	DIQ	Percentile
Verbal Scale	_____	_____	_____	_____	_____	_____
Performance Scale	_____	_____	_____	_____	_____	_____
Full Scale	_____	_____	_____	_____	_____	_____

Wechsler Subscales

Percentile Rank

Scale			
Information	_____	_____	_____
Comprehension	_____	_____	_____
Arithmetic	_____	_____	_____
Similarities	_____	_____	_____
(Digit Span)	_____	_____	_____
Vocabulary	_____	_____	_____
Picture Completion	_____	_____	_____
Picture Arrangement	_____	_____	_____
Block Design	_____	_____	_____
Object Assembly	_____	_____	_____
Digit Symbol (Coding)	_____	_____	_____
(Mazes)	_____	_____	_____
(Animal Pegs)	_____	_____	_____
(Symbol Search)	_____	_____	_____

Form 46   Psychological Autopsy Face Sheet

Date Begun: _____

Date Completed: _____

Subject: _____   Dates Included: _____

Birthdate: _____   Age: _____   Marital Status: S M D W   Children: _____

Religion: _____   Employment: _____   Living Arrangements: _____

Mate: _____

Parents: _____

Sibs: _____

Recent Events: (Date of Termination: _____ _____ A.M. or P.M.)

1. Deaths: _____

2. Anniversaries: _____

3. Marriages: _____

4. Divorces: _____

5. Health Problems: _____

6. Other: _____

Circumstances of Death:

Autopsy Report:

4.75

Form 46a   Psychological Autopsy Face Sheet

Date Begun: _6-14-95_

Date Completed: _7-22-95_

Subject: _Gerston, Betty_   Dates Included: _30 days Pre_

Birthdate: _1-1-23_   Age: _72_   Marital Status: S (M) D W   Children: _3 Females, 1 Male_

Religion: _Baptist_   Employment: _Seamstress_   Living Arrangements: _With Husband_

Mate: _Clyde Gerston, Age 75. (Early Alzheimer's)_

Parents: _Deceased_

Sibs: _2 brothers, 1 sister_

Recent Events: (Date of Termination: _1-3-95_   _6:30_   (A.M.) or P.M.)

1. Deaths: _Brother, 6-91_

2. Anniversaries: _Marriage: June 15, 1947_

3. Marriages: _Son's Marriage June, 1994 (2nd)_

4. Divorces: _Son: May 1993_

5. Health Problems: _Kidney disease. Transplanted 8-93. Successful._

6. Other: _Neighbors report victim and husband have engaged in loud arguments for years._

Circumstances of Death:

Found by husband at 6:30 A.M. 1-3-95. On floor of basement of their home. Bullet wound to right temple area. Husband's .22 caliber pistol found on the washing machine next to the body.

Both husband's and victim's fingerprints on the weapon. Police interview with husband notes he was confused and disoriented. He claims he awakened and was looking for the deceased "to cook me breakfast" and eventually found her in the basement. He called a neighbor on the phone. Mr. Brown, the neighbor, came over, saw the body and called the police and the Gerstons' son.

Autopsy Report:

Apparent time of death 5:30 A.M. Penetrating head wound. Massive haematoma of Right Tempero-Frontal area plus extensive damage to the anterior portions of the cortex. Proximate power burns (non-contact) on right temple.

Form 47   Evaluation of Pre-Terminal Month— Psychological Autopsy

Responder: _____ By: _____ Date of Interview: _____

Relation to Deceased: _____

How Often in Contact with Deceased: _____

_____

_____

Informant's Description of Deceased's Emotional State Prior to Termination: _____

_____

Inquiry:

1. Psychological Pain: _____

_____

2. Frustrated Needs: _____

_____

3. Evidence of Threats: _____

_____

4. Evidence of Plans: _____

_____

5. Evidence of Hopelessness/Helplessness: _____

_____

6. Evidence of Severe Ambivalence/Depression: _____

_____

7. Constricted Thinking: _____

_____

8. Cry for Help: _____

_____

9. Recent Evidence of Sudden Change in Attitude or Behavior: _____

_____

10. Use of Intoxicants: _____

_____

11. Past Attempts: _____

_____

12. Mental Health Treatment: _____

_____

Form 47a   Evaluation of Pre-Terminal Month— Psychological Autopsy

Responder: _Mrs. Ivey Benstrom_   By: _DR._   Date of Interview: _6-16-95_

Relation to Deceased: _Mrs. Gerston was her seamstress._

How Often in Contact with Deceased: _Once or twice a week for the past five years._

Informant's Description of Deceased's Emotional State Prior to Termination:

"On the last 2 or 3 fittings Betty was 'funny.' She seemed 'low.' On her last visit she wanted to give me a ring her mother had given her."

Inquiry:

1. Psychological Pain: _She's been "mopey" for a while._

2. Frustrated Needs: _She was very worried about her mortgage payments and her husband's mental condition._

3. Evidence of Threats: _Not known._

4. Evidence of Plans: _Kept saying "I've got it worked out" during her last visit._

5. Evidence of Hopelessness/Helplessness: _More last month than last week._

6. Evidence of Severe Ambivalence/Depression: _She was low._

7. Constricted Thinking: _She seemed to "drift off" a lot lately._

8. Cry for Help: _"Last month she asked me if I thought she ought to see a doctor about her 'blues.'"_

9. Recent Evidence of Sudden Change in Attitude or Behavior: _"She was 'funny' the last few times she came for fittings."_

10. Use of Intoxicants: _She's always been a drinker._

11. Past Attempts: _I'm not sure. She used to talk about "ending it" now and then._

12. Mental Health Treatment: _Don't know._

Her husband's condition has been bothering her a lot this year. She said she can't take care of him anymore.

Form 48   Psychological Autopsy Interview

Victim: _____ Birthdate: _____

Date of Death: _____ Date of Interview: _____ By: _____

_____ Personal   _____ Telephone   Time—Start: _____ A P   Time—End: _____ A P

Interviewee: _____

Relationship to victim: _____

Contact with victim 30 days prior to death: _____

_____

_____

Victim's appearance and mood: _____

_____

_____

_____

_____

_____

Interviewee's observations of victim:

____ Using alcohol   ____ Using drugs   ____ Depressed

____ Confused   ____ Threatening vengeance   ____ Odd or strange ideas

____ Irrational   ____ Inappropriate affect   ____ Overly optimistic

____ Suicidal ideas   ____ Suicidal threats   ____ Strange behavior

____ Perturbed   ____ Change in dress   ____ Change in routines

____ Angry   ____ Gave things away   ____ Wrote notes or letters

____ Cryptic reassurance that
     all will be well

Other:

— Past attempts:

— Recent anniversaries:

— Religious activity:

Estimate of validity of responses:

Form 49   Final Form for Psychological Autopsy

Most Probable Scenario:

Conclusions:

By: _____

Title: _____

_____

Form 49a   Final Form for Psychological Autopsy

Most Probable Scenario:

1. During the months of November and December of 1994 Mrs. Gerston appeared to her friends, neighbors and employers as increasingly despondent about her husband's deteriorating mental and physical condition.

2. It is reported that she was increasingly perturbed and distressed about her diminishing financial resources and the family's increased indebtedness.

3. She was greatly perturbed by the lack of interest and support from her immediate family.

4. During the month previous to her termination she gave away or attempted to give away some of her prized personal possessions.

5. A regular drinker, her drinking apparently accelerated during December of 1994.

6. The week before she died she told several friends and neighbors that she was "working on a plan to fix everything."

7. The week before Mrs. Gerston's death she was served with a foreclosure notice for long delinquent payments on her home mortgage.

Conclusions:

1. It is more likely than not that Mrs. Gerston's death was a self-termination (suicide).

By: _Dr._____

Title: _Consulting Psychologist_____

_____

Form 50   Visitation Questionnaire

Case: _____   Child(ren): _____

Date: _____   _____

_____

Name of Custodian: _____   Relationship to Child(ren): _____

Current Visitation Arrangement: _____

_____

_____

Your Desired Visitation Schedule: _____

_____

Other Custodian Participants:

A. _____ ☐   D. _____ ☐

B. _____ ☐   E. _____ ☐

C. _____ ☐   F. _____ ☐

Your Preference for Visitation Rights for the Above (Mark Rating in Box):

0	1	2	3	4	5	6
No Visitation Whatsoever	Very Least Allowable by Law	Once or Twice a Year	1 or 2 Weekends per Month	1/Week Overnight	1 Week per Month + Some Holidays	Full Visitation Rights Including Significant Periods of Full-Time Caretaking

Your Most Serious Objections to Other Custodial Participants:

A. _____

_____

B. _____

_____

C. _____

_____

D. _____

_____

E. _____

_____

F. _____

_____

Your Assets as Custodian: _____

_____

Your Liabilities as Custodian: _____

_____

Form 50a   Visitation Questionnaire

Case: _Jones vs. Jones_   Child(ren): _William Jr. (8)_

Date: _4-24-98_   _Mary (5)_

Name of Custodian: _Winifred Jones_   Relationship to Child(ren): _Mother_

Current Visitation Arrangement: _Children in residence with mother. Shared parental responsibility. Father has weekend custody and visitation alternate weekends (Friday 5:00 P.M.–Sunday 5:00 P.M.). Telephone calls 5 P.M. to 6 P.M. daily._

Your Desired Visitation Schedule: _None for father, his new wife or his mother (the paternal grandmother)_

Other Custodian Participants:

A. _William Jones (Father)_   [0]   D. _____   ☐

B. _Debbie Jones (Stepmother)_   [0]   E. _____   ☐

C. _Amanda Jones (Grandmother)_   [1]   F. _____   ☐

Your Preference for Visitation Rights for the Above (Mark Rating in Box):

0	1	2	3	4	5	6
No Visitation Whatsoever	Very Least Allowable by Law	Once or Twice a Year	1 or 2 Weekends per Month	1/Week Overnight	1 Week per Month + Some Holidays	Full Visitation Rights Including Significant Periods of Full-Time Caretaking

Your Most Serious Objections to Other Custodial Participants:

A. _He is a drunk and a wife abuser. I fear he will physically and maybe sexually abuse the children._

B. _She is a bimbo and has a bad influence on the children. She drinks heavily and smokes like a chimney._

C. _She overindulges and spoils the children. She smokes. She tells the children outrageous lies about me._

D. _____

E. _____

F. _____

Your Assets as Custodian: _I'm their mother. I love them. I'm kind and understanding. I spend time with them. I help them with their school work. I don't smoke or drink anymore._

Your Liabilities as Custodian: _Sometimes I'm a little stubborn and want things just so—but it's always in the children's best interests._

Form 51 The Best Interests of the Child—Parent Evaluation Worksheet

Name: _____ Date: _____

Age: _____ Custodial Status: _____

Intelligence:

Work Status:

Personality:

Assets:

Liabilities:

Opportunities:

Specific Recommendations:

Form 51a   The Best Interests of the Child—Parent Evaluation Worksheet

Name: _Winifred Jones_   Date: _5-22-98_

Age: _37_   Custodial Status: _Custodial parent (Biological Mother)_

Intelligence: _72nd Percentile_
High—Average

Work Status: _Beautician—mornings from 9 A.M.—1 P.M._

Personality: _Tendency to labile; histrionic overreaction_

Assets: _Energetic_
Spends time with children
Athletically inclined
Helpful with homework
Encourages creativity

Liabilities: _Bitter attitude toward children's father_
Uncompromising toward children's father
Stubborn
Tends to overreact to minor issues
Dirt-phobic

Opportunities: _Very anxious to improve mothering and parenting skills. Likes to learn about childrearing._
Active in PTA

Specific Recommendations: 1. _Attend parent-effectiveness training._
2. _Attend single-parent support group._
3. _Brief cognitive therapy to help with excess emotionality and phobias._
4. _Opportunity for conference with child development professional._

4.85

Form 52   The Best Interests of the Child—Workup Sheet

Child: _____   Case: _____   Date: _____

Current Arrangement: _____

Intelligence:
    VS _____
    PS _____
    FS _____

Neuropsychology:

Academic:

Personality:

Current Stage:

Next Stage:

Other:

Form 52a   The Best Interests of the Child—Workup Sheet

Child: _William Jones Jr. "Willy"_   Case: _Jones v. Jones_   Date: _5-14-98_

Current Arrangement: _Mother is residential parent. Father visitation alternate weekends_

Intelligence:
VS _118_
PS _114_
FS _117_

Neuropsychology: _Some residual mixed dominance but this seems helpful in his success in soccer._

Academic: _At grade level or above in all areas except math computation. Six months below grade level in arithmetic problem-solving. Need some remedial help._

Personality: _Quiet, slightly withdrawn. Very anxious about parental disharmony. Holds in real feelings. Misses frequent contact with father. Normal sibling rivalry. Very close to maternal grandmother._

Current Stage: _Pre-latency_

Next Stage: _Latency_

Other: _Seems very fearful of saying anything positive about his father in front of his mother. Rapidly developing negative attitudes toward the stepmother as an "interloper." Maintains an inner hope his parents will reconcile. Very threatened and resentful of his sister's growing positive attitudes toward the stepmother._

Form 53   The Best Interests of the Child

Case: _____ v. _____ Date: _____

Child: _____ DOB: _____ Age: _____ Grade: _____ Sex: _____

General Needs:

1. Home:

2. School:

3. Social:

4. Grandparents:

5. Other Relatives:

6. Health Needs:

7. Emotional Needs:

8. Other Needs:

Form 53a   The Best Interests of the Child

Case: _Jones v. Jones_   **Date:** _5-16-98_

Child: _"Willy"_   **DOB:** _9-1-89_   **Age:** _8-7_   **Grade:** _3.8_   **Sex:** _M_

General Needs:

1. Home: _A more positive attitude by the mother toward the father._
   A more tolerant attitude by the mother toward the father's phone calls.

2. School: _Some tutoring in arithmetic problem-solving._

3. Social: _Encourage enrollment in scouts and soccer league._

4. Grandparents: _Encourage continued and regular contacts._

5. Other Relatives: _Set limits on maternal aunt's caustic commentary about the father._

6. Health Needs: _A general physical examination is past due._

7. Emotional Needs: _Some family counseling plus some individual sessions to deal with his conflicts_
   concerning the blended family.

8. Other Needs:

Form 54   Meeting the Best Interests of the Children: Parental Summary

Assets:

Liabilities:

Recommendations:

1. Self-Improvement:

2. Relating to Other Parent:

3. Professional Recommendations:

4. Resolving Future Conflicts:

5. Other:

Form 54a   Meeting the Best Interests of the Children: Parental Summary

Assets:

1. She loves her son.
2. She has signed-up for parent effectiveness training.
3. She is intelligent.
4. She expresses a willingness to work in the best interests of the child.

Liabilities:

1. She is unrelenting in her hostility to Willy's father.
2. She is overly-excitable.

Recommendations:

1. Self-Improvement:

    a. Parent-effectiveness training
    b. Rage-reduction counseling

2. Relating to Other Parent:

    a. Counseling (above)
    b. Clear cut visitation procedures

3. Professional Recommendations:

    a. See above
    b. Parent-effectiveness training for stepfather

4. Resolving Future Conflicts:

    a. Select ombudsman to mediate conflicts

5. Other:

Form 55   Visitation Plan Outline

A. Facts of the Case:

   1. Legal situation and referral source.
   2. Family structure.
   3. Questions to be answered.

B. Best Interests of the Child:

   1. Effects of divorce on children.
   2. Disclaimers.
   3. Responsibilities of parents, attorneys, and court.

C. Evaluations of the Child(ren):

   1. The report(s).
   2. Delineation for the child(ren)s current and anticipated best interests.

D. Evaluations of Parents and Other Visitation Figures:

   1. The reports.
   2. Summary of assets, liabilities, and opportunities in respect to meeting the needs of the child(ren).

E. The Visitation Plan:

   1. Introductory admonitions and limitations.
   2. The role of the primary caretaker in the child(ren)s best interests.
   3. The roles of visitation parties in the child(ren)s best interests.
   4. Logistics:
      a. Time
      b. Place
      c. Environment and territoriality
      d. Place and manner of exchanges
      e. Activities and schedules
      f. Communication during and between visits
   5. Modifications likely to be required as the child(ren) move to new developmental stages.

F. External Auditing:

   1. Understanding and agreement of all parties as to need for auditing.
   2. Selection of external auditor and the developmental evaluator.
   3. Implementing procedures for auditing during crisis or conflict.
   4. Developmental stage evaluations.

Form 56   Standard Paragraphs for Custody or Visitation Plan

The Best Interests of the Children

1. Extensive research in the area of divorce and its effects suggest that all children, regardless of age, are negatively affected by fracturing of the nuclear family. The degree of effect can vary, but the effects are negative. It is clear that the more conflict that exists between the parents, the more stress is likely to fall upon the children.

2. No matter how carefully a marital fracturing is handled, nor how much time is devoted to proper custody and visitation planning, the issue of the children's best interests remains one of great concern. Children of divorce cannot be "totally fixed." No therapy is fully effective. The degree of pain and suffering can be lessened, but this generally requires very close cooperation and communication among the significant parties—the Bar, the Bench, the parents, the community, and others who influence the children.

3. When an issue such as possible child abuse enters the picture, the entire situation is complicated and made more difficult. Although the issue of guilt versus innocence in respect to accused parties is a matter of deep concern, the impact of interrogation, accusation, and the judicial process have far-reaching negative effects on the children. The balance of criminal justice issues versus the best interests of the children is a knotty one and is unlikely to be settled by rhetoric, judicial decision making, or retreat to the moral high ground. The basic rule is that the more the conflict, the more the best interests of the children are badly served.

Form 57   Wisconsin Card Sort

Name: _____   DOB: _____   Age: _____

Date Administered: _____   By: _____

Means & SD of Normals by Age*

Factor:	Score:	< 40 Years		40–49 Years		50–59 Years		> 59 Years	
1. Categories	_____	5.6	(1.0)	4.8	(1.8)	5.6	(1.1)	4.2	(2.0)
2. Errors—Total	_____	21.6	(16.7)	31.0	(27.0)	20.9	(12.8)	44.1	(18.9)
3. Perseverative responses	_____	13.0	(9.1)	19.5	(14.9)	14.8	(9.0)	28.9	(13.7)
4. Nonperseverative errors	_____	11.2	(11.1)	15.1	(15.0)	9.6	(6.2)	19.9	(9.1)
5. Perseverative errors	_____	10.4	(8.0)	16.0	(13.9)	11.3	(6.9)	24.2	(12.8)

Interpretation:

By: _____

*Heaton, R. (1981). *A Manual for the Wisconsin Card-Sorting Test.* Odessa, FL: Psychological Assessment Resources, Inc.

4.94

Form 57a   Wisconsin Card Sort

Name: *Bonner, Pam*   **DOB:** *3-22-40*   **Age:** *57-10*

Date Administered: *1-27-98*   **By:** *PAB*

Means & SD of Normals by Age*

Factor:	Score:	< 40 Years		40–49 Years		50–59 Years		> 59 Years		
1. Categories	3	5.6	(1.0)	4.8	(1.8)	5.6	(1.1)	4.2	(2.0)	2 + Men
2. Errors—Total	65	21.6	(16.7)	31.0	(27.0)	20.9	(12.8)	44.1	(18.9)	3 + Men
3. Perseverative responses	57	13.0	(9.1)	19.5	(14.9)	14.8	(9.0)	28.9	(13.7)	3 + Men
4. Nonperseverative errors	21	11.2	(11.1)	15.1	(15.0)	9.6	(6.2)	19.9	(9.1)	2 + Men
5. Perseverative errors	44	10.4	(8.0)	16.0	(13.9)	11.3	(6.9)	24.2	(12.8)	3 + Men

Interpretation:

Significant deficits. Performance 2–3 standard deviations poorer than age cohorts. Suggests serious deficits in executive functions.

By: *Dr.*

*Heaton, R. (1981). *A Manual for the Wisconsin Card-Sorting Test.* Odessa, FL: Psychological Assessment Resources, Inc.

Form 58 Trails A and B

Name: _____ Date Administered: _____

DOB: _____ Age: _____ By: _____

                                                            *Norms Age: _____

	Time		Time	SD
1. Trails A	_____		_____	_____
2. Trails B	_____		_____	_____

Interpretation:

*Reference: Auch, D. & Yeudall, L. (1983). Normative data for the Halstead-Reitan Neuropsychological tests. *Journal of Clinical Neuropsychology, 5*(3), 221–238.

		Part A			Part B		
Age	*n*	*M*	SD	Range	*M*	SD	Range
15–17	32	23.4	5.9	15.2–39.0	47.7	10.4	25.4–81.0
18–23	76	26.7	9.4	12.0–60.1	51.3	14.6	23.3–101.0
24–32	57	24.3	7.6	11.8–46.0	53.2	15.6	29.1–98.0
33–40	18	27.5	8.3	16.0–52.7	62.1	17.5	39.0–111.0
41–64	10	29.7	8.4	16.5–42.0	73.6	19.4	41.9–102.0

Form 58a   Trails A and B

Name: _Bonner, Pam_   **Date Administered:** _1-27-98_

DOB: _3-22-40_   **Age:** _57-10_   **By:** _PAB_

                                    ***Norms Age:** _41-64_

	Time	Time	SD	
1. Trails A	_39 secs._	_____	_____	_1 + S.D. from M_
2. Trails B	_142 secs._	_____	_____	_3 S.D. from M_

Errors: 0 on A; 1 on Sample B & 1 on B

Interpretation:

Abnormal A & B. Confirms deficiencies in short-term memory and planning ability.

*Reference: Auch, D. & Yeudall, L. (1983). Normative data for the Halstead-Reitan Neuropsychological tests. *Journal of Clinical Neuropsychology, 5*(3), 221–238.

		Part A				Part B		
Age	*n*	*M*	SD	Range		*M*	SD	Range
15–17	32	23.4	5.9	15.2–39.0		47.7	10.4	25.4–81.0
18–23	76	26.7	9.4	12.0–60.1		51.3	14.6	23.3–101.0
24–32	57	24.3	7.6	11.8–46.0		53.2	15.6	29.1–98.0
33–40	18	27.5	8.3	16.0–52.7		62.1	17.5	39.0–111.0
41–64	10	29.7	8.4	16.5–42.0		73.6	19.4	41.9–102.0

Form 59   Hand Dynamometer

Name: _____   Date: _____

Dominant Hand: _____   Physical Condition: _____

Peripheral Problems: _____

Dominant Hand: _____   Nondominant Hand: _____

1. _____Kg.   1. _____Kg.

2. _____Kg.   2. _____Kg.

Average: _____ Kg.   Average: _____ Kg.

Patient's Age: _____   Sex: ____

Dominant Hand Base Rate Mean: _____   S.D.: _____

Nondominant Hand Base Rate Mean: _____   S.D.: _____

Base Rate Norm Study: _____

Interpretation:

Normative Data for the *Dynamometer*.* Stratified by Age and Sex

Males

		Preferred Hand			Nonpreferred Hand		
Age	n	M	SD	Range	M	SD	Range
15–17	17	38.0	8.4	22.2–51.0	35.8	9.6	21.0–57.5
18–23	43	49.7	9.7	30.0–71.2	46.6	9.9	26.7–73.0
24–32	31	51.8	8.1	37.0–65.5	49.6	7.2	30.5–66.0
33–40	12	52.9	8.3	41.0–67.0	51.2	7.9	36.2–62.5
41–64	4	44.5	10.9	30.5–57.0	47.9	11.9	32.0–58.7

Females

Age	n	M	SD	Range	M	SD	Range
15–17	15	28.1	5.0	21.0–37.5	26.3	5.2	17.8–33.5
18–23	29	28.8	7.8	8.5–43.8	26.4	6.2	13.5–38.0
24–32	24	34.4	9.2	20.5–64.7	30.2	6.8	20.5–49.5
33–40	6	27.7	3.2	23.0–31.5	28.6	3.1	25.2–33.5
41–64	6	28.0	6.2	18.7–37.5	24.1	6.8	16.7–36.5

*Kilogram average of two trials.

By: _____   Date: _____

Auch, D. & Yeudall, L. (1983). Normative data for the Halstead-Reitan neuropsychological tests. *Journal of Clinical Neuropsychology, 5*(3), 221–238.

Form 59a Hand Dynamometer

Name: _Walker, Tom_ _____ **Date:** _2-17-98_

Dominant Hand: _Right_ _____ **Physical Condition:** _Mobile_ _____

Peripheral Problems: _MVA-CNS Problems_ _____

Dominant Hand: _Right_ _____   **Nondominant Hand:** _Left_ _____

1. _47.5_ **Kg.**   1. _46_ **Kg.**

2. _49.5_ **Kg.**   2. _47_ **Kg.**

Average: _48_ **Kg.**   **Average:** _46.5_ **Kg.**

Patient's Age: _15-0_   **Sex:** _M_

Dominant Hand Base Rate Mean: _38.0_   **S.D.:** _8.4_ _____

                                             Male Ages 15–17 _____

Nondominant Hand Base Rate Mean: _35.8_   **S.D.:** _9.6_ _____

Base Rate Norm Study: _Auch & Yeudall_ _____

Interpretation:

No abnormality. Within normal limits.

Normative Data for the *Dynamometer.** Stratified by Age and Sex

Males

		Preferred Hand			Nonpreferred Hand		
Age	**n**	**M**	**SD**	**Range**	**M**	**SD**	**Range**
15–17	17	38.0	8.4	22.2–51.0	35.8	9.6	21.0–57.5
18–23	43	49.7	9.7	30.0–71.2	46.6	9.9	26.7–73.0
24–32	31	51.8	8.1	37.0–65.5	49.6	7.2	30.5–66.0
33–40	12	52.9	8.3	41.0–67.0	51.2	7.9	36.2–62.5
41–64	4	44.5	10.9	30.5–57.0	47.9	11.9	32.0–58.7

Females

Age	**n**	**M**	**SD**	**Range**	**M**	**SD**	**Range**
15–17	15	28.1	5.0	21.0–37.5	26.3	5.2	17.8–33.5
18–23	29	28.8	7.8	8.5–43.8	26.4	6.2	13.5–38.0
24–32	24	34.4	9.2	20.5–64.7	30.2	6.8	20.5–49.5
33–40	6	27.7	3.2	23.0–31.5	28.6	3.1	25.2–33.5
41–64	6	28.0	6.2	18.7–37.5	24.1	6.8	16.7–36.5

*Kilogram average of two trials.

By: _E.R._   **Date:** _2-18-98_

Auch, D. & Yeudall, L. (1983). Normative data for the Halstead-Reitan neuropsychological tests. *Journal of Clinical Neuropsychology, 5*(3), 221–238.

Form 60   Formulae for Estimating Premorbid WAIS-R Scores

1. Estimated Verbal IQ =

    54.23 + 0.49 (Age) + 1.92 (Sex) + 4.24 (Race) + 1.89 (Occupation) + 5.25 (Education) + 1.24 (U-R Residence)

    Standard Error of Estimate = 11.79

2. Estimated Performance IQ =

    61.58 + 0.31 (Age) + 1.09 (Sex) + 4.95 (Race) + 3.75 (Education) + 1.54 (Occupation) + 0.59 (Region)

    Standard Error of Estimate = 13.25

3. Estimated Full Scale IQ =

    54.96 + 0.47 (Age) + 1.76 (Sex) + 4.71 (Race) + 5.02 (Education) + 1.89 (Occupation) + 0.59 (Region)

    Standard Error of Estimate = 12.14

Variables

Sex	Race	Region	Residence	Occupation	Age	Completed Education
Female = 1	Black = 1	South = 1	Rural = 1	Prof. & Tech. = 6	16–17 = 1	0–7 = 1
Male = 2	Other = 2	N. Central = 2	Urban = 2	Mgrs., Owners, &	18–19 = 2	8 = 2
	White = 3	Western = 3		Officials = 5	20–24 = 3	9–11 = 3
		N. East = 4		Skilled = 4	25–34 = 4	12 = 4
				Not in Labor	35–44 = 5	13–15 = 5
				Force = 3	45–54 = 6	16 & up = 6
				Semi-Skilled = 2	55–64 = 7	
				Unskilled = 1	65–69 = 8	
					70–74 = 9	

IQs above 120 tend to be under-estimated.

IQs below 69 tend to be over-estimated.

Source: Barona, A., Reynolds, C., & Chastain, R. (1984). A demographically based index of pre-morbid intelligence for the WAIS-R. *Journal of Consulting and Clinical Psychology, 52*(5), 885–887.

Form 60a   Worksheet for Estimating Premorbid WAIS-R Scores

Verbal IQ:		Performance IQ:		Full Scale IQ:	
	54.23		61.59		54.96
0.49 x Age ____ = ____		0.31 x Age ____ = ____		0.47 x Age ____ = ____	
1.92 x Sex ____ = ____		1.09 x Sex ____ = ____		1.76 x Sex ____ = ____	
4.24 x Race ____ = ____		4.95 x Race ____ = ____		4.71 x Race ____ = ____	
1.89 x Occup ____ = ____		3.75 x Educ ____ = ____		5.02 x Educ ____ = ____	
5.25 x Educ ____ = ____		1.54 x Occup ____ = ____		1.89 x Occup ____ = ____	
1.24 x Ur/Ru ____ = ____		0.59 x Region ____ = ____		0.59 x Region ____ = ____	
Estimated IQ: ____		Estimated IQ: ____		Estimated IQ: ____	
(Standard Error – 11.79)		(Standard Error – 13.25)		(Standard Error – 12.14)	

Variables

Sex	Race	Region	Residence	Occupation	Age	Completed Education
Female = 1	Black = 1	South = 1	Rural = 1	Prof. & Tech. = 6	16–17 = 1	0–7 = 1
Male = 2	Other = 2	N. Central = 2	Urban = 2	Mgrs., Owners, &	18–19 = 2	8 = 2
	White = 3	Western = 3		Officials = 5	20–24 = 3	9–11 = 3
		N. East = 4		Skilled = 4	25–34 = 4	12 = 4
				Not in Labor	35–44 = 5	13–15 = 5
				Force = 3	45–54 = 6	16 & up = 6
				Semi-Skilled = 2	55–64 = 7	
				Unskilled = 1	65–69 = 8	
					70–74 = 9	

IQs above 120 tend to be under-estimated.
IQs below 69 tend to be over-estimated.

Source: Barona, A., Reynolds, C., & Chastain, R. (1984). A demographically based index of pre-morbid intelligence for the WAIS-R. *Journal of Consulting and Clinical Psychology, 52*(5), 885–887.

4.101

Form 61   MMPI Comparison

Name: _____   Date: _____

Scale	Date/Test	Date/Test	Date/Test	Date/Test
L				
F				
K				
Hs				
D				
Hy				
Pd				
Mf				
Pa				
Pt				
Sc				
Ma				
Si				
F-K				
VRIN				
TRIN				
FB* Scale				

* Lees-Haley, P. (1992). Efficacy of MMPI-2 validity scales and MCMI-II modifier scales for detecting spurious PTSD claims: F, F-K, fake bad scale, ego strength, subtle-obvious subscales, DIS, and DEB. *Journal of Clinical Psychology, 48*(5), 681–689.

* Lees-Haley, P., English, L., & Glenn, W. (1991). A fake bad scale on the MMPI-2 for personal injury claimants. *Psychological Reports, 68,* 203–210.

Form 62   Probability of Malingering Checklist

The more of these conditions that exist, the more likely that the individual being examined is simulating, malingering, or being deceptive.

_____ 1. The individual presents the symptoms in a histrionic or very dramatic manner.

_____ 2. The individual cannot engage in meaningful compensatory work but can engage in leisure activities.

_____ 3. The reason for the evaluation is medico-legal.

_____ 4. The individual shows a lack of cooperation in participating in the evaluation, scheduling, or appearing on time.

_____ 5. There is a history of character pathology in the behavior of the individual before the alleged event.

_____ 6. There is a marked discrepancy between the claimed stress, disease or disorder, and objective signs or measurements of the conditions.

_____ 7. The description of the event is embellished.

_____ 8. Relatives seem to have a vested interest in embellishing the event.

_____ 9. On the MMPI, scales 4 and/or 9 are significantly elevated.

_____ 10. On the Millon Clinical Multiaxial Inventory, the anti-social personality scale has a base rate above 85.

_____ 11. The individual is able to do things at home and perform tasks in his or her environment that he or she claims not to be able to do in a work setting.

_____ 12. The symptoms presented are blatantly absurd in respect to what ordinarily would be found in the supposed condition.

_____ 13. The individual presents symptom combinations that are either very rare or unknown in the literature.

_____ 14. The condition developed very suddenly.

_____ 15. The individual presents symptoms that ordinarily are rarely or never found together.

_____ 16. If the individual when he is unobserved behaves in ways that he claims he cannot do, this suggests that the malingering is conscious and intentional.

_____ 17. The individual performs very badly on a very simple psychological test after she is told that the test is extremely difficult.

_____ 18. Scale 4 of the MMPI exceeds Scale 3, suggesting conscious control of the symptomatology.

_____ 19. If Scale 3 of the MMPI exceeds Scale 4, the clinician should explore the possibility that malingering or simulation may be an unconscious hysterical symptom.

Price, J. R. (1991). _Deception and Malingering._ Continuing Education Workshop, Psychological Seminars.

Form 63 Factors That Increase Potential Incredibility and Distortion in the Testimony of Children

No.	Factor	Yes	Questionable	No
1.	Age of child (pre-school more than children of 8 years or older).	___	___	___
2.	Parental conflict.	___	___	___
3.	Accused not a stranger.	___	___	___
4.	Number of interviews (rehearsal effect).	___	___	___
5.	Number of interviewers (greater number equals more likelihood of distortion, bias, expectancy).	___	___	___
6.	Initial interviewers lack skill and training in interviewing.	___	___	___
7.	Interviews are suggestive, and there's a variability of the interviewer's agenda and expectations for the child.	___	___	___
8.	When the child acts uncertain, the interviewer presses for the child to make an absolute decision.	___	___	___
9.	Misleading questions by interviewers.	___	___	___
10.	Leading questions by interviewers.	___	___	___
11.	The longer the time between the alleged event and the interview, the more likely distortion.	___	___	___
12.	The more stressful the event on which the child is reporting, the more anxious the child, the more likely the report will be distorted or incredible.	___	___	___
13.	The child who is exposed to the stress of subsequent interviews and events (cumulative effect) is likely to be more and more incredible in their descriptions.	___	___	___
14.	The more interventions, the more distortion (therapy, parental discussion, interested friends, participation in sexual abuse therapy, participation in support groups, and so forth).	___	___	___
15.	The record shows significant changes in extent and details of alleged event from first through last interview.	___	___	___
16.	The accusing party has demonstrated vengefulness, malice, and other negative attitudes toward the party being accused.	___	___	___
17.	The accusing parent has a strong emotional tie, connection, and tendency to influence the attitudes and emotionality of the child.	___	___	___
18.	The child has prior knowledge of sexual matters or events and tends to be more sophisticated in these areas than other young children of similar age.	___	___	___
19.	Professional persons, either as diagnosticians or therapists make the decision that abuse is real and has occurred before a careful investigation and determination takes place.	___	___	___
20.	Pre-trial therapy based on the assumption that the child has really been sexually abused.	___	___	___

Blau, T., & Blau, R. (1988). The competence and credibility of children as witnesses. In J. Reese & J. Horn (Eds.), *Policy psychology: Operational assistance.* Washington, DC: U.S. Department of Justice, U.S. Government Printing Office.

Doris, J. (Ed.). (1991). *The suggestibility of children's recollections.* Washington, DC: American Psychological Association.

Wakefield, H., & Underwager, R. (1990). Personality characteristics of parents making false accusations of sexual abuse in custody disputes. *Issues in Child Abuse Accusations, 2*(3), 121–136.

Name: _____   **Date:** _____

Subtest	Number of Errors
I	_____
II	_____

Normative Scores (Number of Errors)*

	Malingerers		Brain Injured		Controls	
	M	**(SD)**	**M**	**(SD)**	**M**	**(SD)**
Subtest I	2.4	(2.5)	0.0	(0.2)	0.0	(0.0)
Subtest II	5.1	(4.7)	0.4	(0.5)	0.1	(0.3)

Hit rate for the above is 92.2%; false positives = 0%; false negatives = 27%.

Source: Tenhula, W., & Sweet, J. (1996). Double cross-validation of the Booklet Category Test in detecting malingered traumatic brain injury. *The Clinical Neuropsychologist, 10,* 104–116.

Form 64a   Scoring Sheet for Detecting Malingering on the Booklet Category Test

Name: _Smith, Elvira_   **Date:** _6-23-98_

Subtest	Number of Errors
I	3
II	8

Normative Scores (Number of Errors)*

	Malingerers		Brain Injured		Controls	
	M	(SD)	M	(SD)	M	(SD)
Subtest I	2.4	(2.5)	0.0	(0.2)	0.0	(0.0)
Subtest II	5.1	(4.7)	0.4	(0.5)	0.1	(0.3)

These results suggest malingering, deception, or "Faking Bad."

Hit rate for the above is 92.2%; false positives = 0%; false negatives = 27%.

Source: Tenhula, W., & Sweet, J. (1996). Double cross-validation of the Booklet Category Test in detecting malingered traumatic brain injury. _The Clinical Neuropsychologist, 10,_ 104–116.

Form 65 Scoring Sheet for Detection of Malingering on the Luria-Nebraska Neuropsychological Battery

Name: _____ Date: _____

<u>Formula</u>: Items A Scores > Items B Scores = Likely malingering*

A Scores		B Scores	
Item	**Score**	**Item**	**Score**
3 (x 2)	_____	132	_____
4	_____	170	_____
44	_____	173	_____
48	_____	174	_____
64	_____	187	_____
66	_____	192	_____
67	_____	199	_____
69	_____	217	_____
71	_____	221	_____
101	_____	223	_____
112	_____	225	_____
160	_____	239	_____
261	_____	241	_____
Total A	_____	**Total B**	_____

_____ A < B   _____ A > B (Likely malingering)

Source: McKinzey, R., Podd, M., Krehbiel, M., Mensch, A., & Trombka, C. (1997). Detection of malingering on the Luria-Nebraska Neuropsychological Battery: An initial and cross-validation. *Archives of Clinical Neuropsychology, 12,* 505–512.

4.107

Form 65a   Scoring Sheet for Detection of Malingering on the Luria-Nebraska Neuropsychological Battery

Name: _Smith, Elvira_   **Date:** _6-23-98_

Formula: **Items A Scores > Items B Scores = Likely malingering***

A Scores		B Scores	
Item	**Score**	**Item**	**Score**
3 (x 2)	6	132	1
4	1	170	0
44	2	173	0
48	1	174	2
64	1	187	1
66	1	192	0
67	2	199	0
69	2	217	1
71	1	221	0
101	2	223	0
112	2	225	1
160	1	239	1
261	1	241	1
Total A	23	**Total B**	8

_____ A < B   __X__ A > B (Likely malingering)

Source: McKinzey, R., Podd, M., Krehbiel, M., Mensch, A., & Trombka, C. (1997). Detection of malingering on the Luria-Nebraska Neuropsychological Battery: An initial and cross-validation. _Archives of Clinical Neuropsychology, 12,_ 505–512.

Form 66   Scoring Sheet for the Identification of Malingered Head Injury on the Wechsler Adult Intelligence Scale—Revised

Name: _____   **Date:** _____

WAIS-R

Age-Corrected Scale Scores

Vocabulary – Digit span = Difference score

_____ - _____ = _____

Probability of Malingering Classification

Vocabulary-Digit Span Difference Score	Probability of Malingering
10	.99
9	.95
8	.90
—	.85
7	.80
6	.75
5	.70
4	.60
3	.60
2	.55
—	.50
1	.45
0	.40
-1	.35
-2	.30
-3	.25
-4	.20
—	.15
-5	.10
-6	.05
-7	.01

Source: Mittenberg, W., Therous-Fichera, S., Zielinski, R., & Heilbronner, R. (1995). Identification of malingered head injury on the Wechsler Adult Intelligence Scale—Revised. *Professional Psychology: Research and Practice, 26,* 491.

4.109

Form 66a   Scoring Sheet for the Identification of Malingered Head Injury on the Wechsler Adult Intelligence Scale—Revised

Name: _Smith, Elvira_   **Date:** _6-23-98_

WAIS-R

Age-Corrected Scale Scores

Vocabulary – Digit span = Difference score

_10_ - _2_ = _+8_

Probability of Malingering Classification

Vocabulary-Digit Span Difference Score	Probability of Malingering
10	.99
9	.95
8	.90
—	.85
7	.80
6	.75
5	.70
4	.60
3	.60
2	.55
—	.50
1	.45
0	.40
-1	.35
-2	.30
-3	.25
-4	.20
—	.15
-5	.10
-6	.05
-7	.01

Source: Mittenberg, W., Therous-Fichera, S., Zielinski, R., & Heilbronner, R. (1995). Identification of malingered head injury on the Wechsler Adult Intelligence Scale—Revised. *Professional Psychology: Research and Practice, 26,* 491.

4.110

Form 67   A Malingering Index for the Wechsler Memory Scale—Revised

Name: _____   Date: _____

General memory – Attention/Concentration = Difference score

(Index scores) _____ - _____ = _____

Probability of Malingering = _____

Probability of Malingering Classification

General Memory Attention/Concentration Score	Probability of Malingering
35	.99
34	.98
—	.97
33	.96
32	.95
—	.94
31	.93
30	.92
29	.91
—	.90
25	.85
22	.80
19	.75
15	.70
12	.65
9	.60
5	.55
2	.50

Sources: Mittenberg, W., Azrin, R., Millsaps, C., & Heilbronner, R. (1993). Identification of malingered head injury on the Wechsler Memory Scale-Revised. *Psychological Assessment, 5*(1), 34–40.
Iverson, G. Slick, D., & Franzen, M. (1996, October & November). Evaluation of a WMS-R malingering index in a non-litigating clinical sample. *Archives of Clinical Neuropsychology, 12,* 341.

Form 67a   A Malingering Index for the Wechsler Memory Scale—Revised

Name: _Smith, Elvira_   **Date:** _6-23-98_

General memory – Attention/Concentration = Difference score

(Index scores) _104_ - _67_ = _37_

Probability of Malingering = _99+_

Probability of Malingering Classification

General Memory-Attention/Concentration Score	Probability of Malingering
35	.99
34	.98
—	.97
33	.96
32	.95
—	.94
31	.93
30	.92
29	.91
—	.90
25	.85
22	.80
19	.75
15	.70
12	.65
9	.60
5	.55
2	.50

Sources: Mittenberg, W., Azrin, R., Millsaps, C., & Heilbronner, R. (1993). Identification of malingered head injury on the Wechsler Memory Scale-Revised. *Psychological Assessment, 5*(1), 34–40.

Iverson, G. Slick, D., & Franzen, M. (1996, October & November). Evaluation of a WMS-R malingering index in a non-litigating clinical sample. *Archives of Clinical Neuropsychology, 12,* 341.

Form 68   Lees-Haley Fake Bad Scale (FBS) for the MMPI-2

Name: _____   Date: _____

True (Check if item answered true):

11 ___,   18 ___,   28 ___,   30 ___,   31 ___,   39 ___,   40 ___,   44 ___,   59 ___,

111 ___,   252 ___,   274 ___,   325 ___,   339 ___,   464 ___,   469 ___,   505 ___,   506 ___

Total: ____

False (Check if item answered false):

12 ___,   41 ___,   57 ___,   58 ___,   81 ___,   110 ___,   117 ___,   152 ___,   164 ___,

176 ___,   224 ___,   227 ___,   248 ___,   249 ___,   250 ___,   255 ___,   264 ___,   284 ___,

362 ___,   373 ___,   419 ___,   433 ___,   496 ___,   561 ___

Total: ____

Total of Checked True and False Responses: _____

Source: Lees-Haley, P. (1992). Efficacy of MMPI-2 validity scales and MCMI-II modifier scales for detecting spurious PTSD claims: F, F-k, fake bad scale, ego strength, subtle-obvious subscales, DIS, and DEB. *Journal of Clinical Psychology, 48*(5), 681–689.
Lees-Haley, P., English, L., & Glenn, W. (1991). A fake bad scale on the MMPI-2 for personal injury claimants. *Psychological Reports, 68,* 203–210.
Notes: Males: cutoff is ‡ 24, 75% pseudo PTSD and 96% controls correctly classified. Females: cutoff is ‡ 26, 74% pseudoPTSD and 92% controls correctly classified. Cutoff of 20, 96% hit rate for malingerers.

Form 68a   Lees-Haley Fake Bad Scale (FBS) for the MMPI-2

Name: _Smith, Elvira_   **Date:** _6-23-98_

True (Check if item answered true):

11 ✓,   18 ___,   28 ✓,   30 ✓,   31 ✓,   39 ___,   40 ✓,   44 ___,   59 ___,

111 ___,   252 ✓,   274 ✓,   325 ✓,   339 ✓,   464 ✓,   469 ✓,   505 ___,   506 ✓

Total: _12_

False (Check if item answered false):

12 ✓,   41 ___,   57 ✓,   58 ___,   81 ___,   110 ✓,   117 ✓,   152 ___,   164 ✓,

176 ___,   224 ✓,   227 ___,   248 ✓,   249 ___,   250 ✓,   255 ___,   264 ✓,   284 ___,

362 ✓,   373 ✓,   419 ✓,   433 ___,   496 ✓,   561 ✓

Total: _14_

Total of Checked True and False Responses: _26_

Source: Lees-Haley, P. (1992). Efficacy of MMPI-2 validity scales and MCMI-II modifier scales for detecting spurious PTSD claims: F, F-k, fake bad scale, ego strength, subtle-obvious subscales, DIS, and DEB. *Journal of Clinical Psychology, 48*(5), 681–689. Lees-Haley, P., English, L., & Glenn, W. (1991). A fake bad scale on the MMPI-2 for personal injury claimants. *Psychological Reports, 68*, 203–210.
Notes: Males: cutoff is ‡ 24, 75% pseudo PTSD and 96% controls correctly classified. Females: cutoff is ‡ 26, 74% pseudo PTSD and 92% controls correctly classified. Cutoff of 20, 96% hit rate for malingerers.

Form 69   Invalidity/Fake Bad/Exaggeration/ Malingering Profile

Name: _____   Date: _____

Examiner: _____

	Probability:				
	V. Low	**Low**	**Equivocal**	**High**	**V. High**
	1	**25**	**50**	**75**	**100**

1. F = _____

2. F-K = _____

3. FbS = _____

4. 15-Item = _____

5. Mittenberg WAIS-R = _____

6. Mittenberg WMS-R = _____

7. Rogers SIRs = _____

_____

_____

_____

8. Hiscock = _____

9. Booklet Category Test = _____

10. Luria-Nebraska = _____

11. _____

_____

_____

Summary:

Form 69a   Invalidity/Fake Bad/Exaggeration/Malingering Profile

Name: _Smith, Elvira_ **Date:** _6-23-98_

Examiner: _D. R._

Probability:

	V. Low 1	Low 25	Equivocal 50	High 75	V. High 100
1. F = __85__			X		
2. F-K = __+8__			X		
3. FbS = __26__				X	
4. 15-Item = __7__					X
5. Mittenberg WAIS-R = __+8__					X
6. Mittenberg WMS-R = __37__					X
7. Rogers SIRs = _____					
_____					
_____					
_____					
8. Hiscock = _____				X	
9. Booklet Category Test = __3 + 8__				X	
10. Luria-Nebraska = _A-23 B-8_					
_____					
_____					
_____					

Summary:

High probability that test scores demonstrating neuropsychological deficit and psychopathology are exaggerated and invalid.

Chapter 5

Forms for Deposition and Trial Preparation

FORM 70
Depositions and Court Appearances

In federal cases, and increasingly in state litigation, the expert witness is required to present to opposing counsel, usually at the time of the deposition, a list of cases in which he or she has been involved during the past 4 or 5 years.

Knowing this, the forensic psychologists would be wise to set up this form on a computer format and add cases as they occur so that a 4- or 5-year list can be readily available. The initial effort to develop such a list is a tedious task, but one that is necessary. Once the format is put on the computer, and the initial case record is in place, it is relatively simple to keep it up to date.

Form 70a presents such a form covering a 4-year period of forensic activity for Dr. Jones.

FORM 71
Distribution of Forensic Cases

During the course of a deposition and sometimes during trial, the expert witness will be asked to summarize his or her deposition and trial experience. Form 71 presents a format that can be used for this purpose. Form 71a shows an actual distribution of forensic cases for a forensic psychologist.

FORM 72
Time Distribution

It is not unusual for a psychologist to be asked when serving as an expert how their clinical time is distributed. Form 72 offers a format for calculating this activity. Form 72a shows an actual time distribution.

FORM 73
Deposition and Conference Record

During the course of any forensic case, there will be conferences and depositions scheduled. The forensic expert may be asked at some point during the proceedings to describe such meetings, when they occurred and with whom. They may be asked how much time was spent on these activities. Form 73 presents a format for making such material easily available in the case folder. Form 73a presents this form filled for a particular case.

FORM 74
Rules of the Road for the Expert
Witness at Trial

Form 74 presents a series of Do's and Don'ts to help the forensic expert make the best possible presentation and to serve in the most efficient, ethical, and thorough manner. At first, the expert should go over this checklist with each deposition and each court appearance. After some time, it will be automatic that the expert checks himself or herself before engaging in a forensic case.

FORM 75
Day in Court Checklist

Before making a court appearance, it would be wise for the forensic expert to be sure that everything has been done that was necessary to support an effective presentation. Form 75 is a checklist that is helpful in insuring that all is well before going to court.

Form 70   Depositions and Court Appearances

Date	C/ CI	Case Style	D/T*	Jurisdiction	AC/ P/D*

* CI–Civil, C–Criminal, D–Deposition, T–Testimony, AC–Amicus Curia, D–Defendant, P–Plaintiff or Prosecution.

Form 70a   Dr. Jones: Depositions and Court Appearances

Date	C/CI	Case Style	D/T*	Jurisdiction	AC/P/D*
1995					
4/10	C	State of FL v. Freeman	D	Circuit Court of Pinellas Co., FL	D
5/20	C	State of FL v. Scoggins	D	12th Judicial Circuit, Sarasota, FL	P
5/23	C	State of FL v. Scoggins	T	Same as above	P
6/5	C	State of FL v. Gonzales	T	Same as above	P
6/25	CI	Allen et al. v. Rubin et al.	D	Superior Court of State of CA, San Bernardino Central District	P
7/3	C	State of FL v. Turner	T	14th Judicial Circuit, Bay Co., FL	D
7/5	CI	Allen et al. v. Rubin et al.	T	Previously listed	P
7/23	CI	Chancey v. Venture Construction	D	15th Judicial Circuit, West Palm Beach, FL	P
7/24	CI	Rebecca Tilley	D	State Court of Bibb Co., GA	P
8/17	C	State of FL v. Norwood	D	14th Judicial Circuit, Bay Co., FL	D
8/20	CI	Noel v. Noel	T	10th Judicial Circuit of FL, Guardian Ad Litem Program	AC
9/9	CI	Smith v. Foulk	D	Circuit Court of Polk Co., FL	P
10/30	CI	Smith v. Foulk	D	Same as above	P
11/18	CI	Schubert v. Holt et al.	D	13th Judicial Circuit, Hillsborough Co., FL	P
12/30	CI	Rebekah Woodruff	D	15th Judicial Circuit, Palm Beach Co., FL	P
1996					
3/2	CI	Kelly v. Hardy	D	9th Judicial Circuit, Orange Co., FL	P
3/13	CI	Cunningham et al. v. Prince et al.	D	U.S. Dist. Court for the N. Dist. of TX, Dallas Div.	P
3/31	C	State of FL v. Richards	T	5th Judicial Circuit, Lake Co., FL	D
4/7	C	State of FL v. Richards	T	Same as above	D
4/26	C	State of FL v. Bundy	D	12th Judicial Circuit, Sarasota Co., FL	P
5/14	CI	Orren v. Calvert	T	Same as above	P
6/15	CI	Pepe v. Salzberg et al.	D	17th Judicial Circuit, Broward Co., FL	P
7/2	CI	Patricia Smithpeters	D	12th Judicial Circuit, Sarasota Co., FL	P
8/4	CI	Orren v. Calvert	D	Same as above	P
9/24	CI	Orren v. Calvert	T	Same as above	P
1997					
2/2	CI	McMillian v. Hattaway	D	U.S. Dist. Court, N. Dist. of FL, Pensacola Division	P
2/24	CI	Cadiz v. Continental Casualty Co.	D	13th Circuit Court, Hillsborough Co., FL	P
3/1	CI	McMillian v. Hattaway	T	Previously listed	D
5/13	CI	CMT Holding v. Marilyn Motto	D	15th Judicial Circuit, Palm Beach Co., FL	D
5/27	CI	McPheron v. Kelly-Springfield	D	5th Judicial Circuit, Lake Co., FL	P
7/5	CI	Allen et al. v. Rubin et al.	T	Previously listed	P
9/27	CI	CMT Holding v. Marilyn Motto	T	Previously listed	P
11/29	CI	Macquarrie v. Venture	D	5th Judicial Circuit, Marion Co., FL	P
12/20 & 21	CI	Macquarrie v. Venture	T	Same as above	P
1998					
1/21	CI	William Bitter	D	9th Judicial Circuit, Orange Co., FL	P
4/19	C	James David Carter v. Dutton et al.	D	U.S. Dist. Court, E. Dist. of TN, N.E. Division	D
6/2	CI	Blunt v. Oca	D	12th Judicial Circuit, Sarasota Co., FL	D
6/16	CI	William Bitter	T	Previously listed	P
9/20	C	State of FL v. Terry Taylor	T	12th Judicial Circuit, Sarasota Co., FL	AC

* CI–Civil, C–Criminal, D–Deposition, T–Testimony, AC–Amicus Curia, D–Defendant, P–Plaintiff or Prosecution.

Form 71   Distribution of Forensic Cases

Year	Depos	Trials	Criminal	Civil	P	D	AC

Form 71a   Distribution of Forensic Cases

Year	Depos	Trials	Criminal	Civil	P	D	AC
1992	6	4	3	7	8	2	0
1993	5	4	0	9	6	3	0
1994	5	4	2	7	4	4	1
1995	5	2	2	5	3	4	0
1996	2	4	2	4	1	5	0
1997	3	2	3	1	2	2	0

Form 72   Time Distribution

The following time distribution is the monthly average for the first five months of [year]. These figures vary from week to week, month to month, and year to year.

Function	Hours per Month	Percent of Time
Psychotherapy		
Assessment		
Training		
Police		
Research		
Forensic		
Writing		
Administration		
Other		

Form 72a   Time Distribution

The following time distribution is the monthly average for the first five months of 1998. These figures vary from week to week, month to month, and year to year.

Function	Hours per Month	Percent of Time
Psychotherapy	34	17%
Assessment	30	15
Training	14	6
Police	30	15
Research	36	18
Forensic	24	11
Writing	22	10
Administration	19	9
Other		

Form 73   Deposition and Conference Record

Case: _____

Date	Purpose	Present	Time

Trial Information:

Form 73a   Deposition and Conference Record

Case: _State v. Greenley_

Date	Purpose	Present	Time
1-7-98	Pre-deposition conference	District Attorney Brown	2:00–2:30 P.M.
1-7-98	Deposition	District Attorney Brown, defendant's attorneys McKay and Phelps	2:30–5:00 P.M.
2-4-98	Pre-trial conference	District Attorney Brown and Assistant District Attorney Flaherty	10:30–11:45 A.M.

Trial Information: _Trial to begin on February 23rd. Dr. probably will go on February 25th._

Form 74   Rules of the Road for the Expert Witness at Trial

_____ DO base opinion on multiple data sources.

_____ DO be prepared to cite reviews, studies, or other corroboration of techniques used in assessment.

_____ DO have citations from references to support choice of instruments.

_____ DO answer "I don't know" when this is the truest answer.

_____ DO avoid answering the ultimate question whenever possible.

_____ DO include contrarian views when explaining data on test results.

_____ DO be mindful of the implications of _Frye v. U.S._ and _Daubert v. Dow Pharmaceuticals_ when formulating an opinion.

_____ DO expect opposing counsel to do his/her homework and to challenge expert opinion.

_____ DO expect retaining counsel to obtain all appropriate records that would be helpful to the expert.

_____ DO give a lecture if opposing counsel asks a general question in an area where you are knowledgeable.

_____ DO ask for more details when opposing counsel poses a hypothetical question that is not absolutely clear to the expert.

_____ DO NOT formulate an opinion clearly at odds with reliable factual behavioral observations.

_____ DON'T lose your temper when challenged—in court or at deposition.

_____ DON'T attempt to guess or estimate what an attorney is asking, ask for clarification before answering.

_____ DO NOT be humorous when giving sworn testimony.

_____ DO NOT be pompous or patronizing when giving sworn testimony.

_____ DON'T be complicated or steeped in professional or scientific jargon when giving sworn testimony.

_____ NEVER speculate or guess when giving sworn testimony.

_____ DO NOT cite your clinical experience as a sole basis of an opinion.

_____ DON'T speak rapidly.

_____ TRY NOT TO be threatened by attorneys implying that the absence of definitive research is evidence.

_____ DO NOT testify outside your own expertise, qualifications or experience.

_____ DO NOT advise lawyers on trial strategy.

_____ DO NOT advocate with opposing counsel.

_____ NEVER disregard a judge's instructions or questions.

_____ NEVER be late for court.

_____ ALWAYS stand when the judge stands.

_____ DO NOT believe that jurors are "dumb."

_____ DO NOT dress unattractively or inappropriately when testifying.

_____ DON'T sit in the courtroom before or after testifying without the permission of retaining counsel.

_____ NEVER talk with witnesses, attorneys, or litigants on the opposing side without the retaining attorney's permission and presence.

Form 75   Day in Court Checklist

Preliminary

- [ ] File complete
- [ ] Scoring checked
- [ ] Charts prepared
- [ ] Preparation to respond to *Daubert v. Dow* challenges

- [ ] Extraneous documents removed
- [ ] Pretrial conference with retaining attorney
- [ ] Back-up material indexed

Day Before Trial

- [ ] Briefcase packed
- [ ] Deposition reviewed
- [ ] Time and place checked with retaining attorney's assistant

- [ ] Best parking option identified
- [ ] Written report reviewed
- [ ] Stress inoculation for evening before appearance

Day of Trial

- [ ] Proper attire
- [ ] Arrive 10 minutes early
- [ ] Announce presence via the bailiff
- [ ] Avoid all communication with other witnesses, the press, or opposing counsel

- [ ] Shine shoes
- [ ] Pack something to read while waiting
- [ ] Do **not** review file while waiting

Following Testimony

- [ ] Thank judge before stepping down
- [ ] Two weeks post-trial call attorney and request review of your performance

- [ ] Return to office and prepare final invoice
- [ ] Check with retaining attorney to decide whether review material should be kept on file, returned or destroyed

Chapter 6

Miscellaneous Forms

FORM 76
Notice That Test Materials Require
Qualified Reviewer

In the course of forensic work, the expert is going to be asked to forward not only copies of his or her report, but also raw data. Most states and certainly the American Psychological Association advise that raw test data be sent only to qualified individuals. Form 76 is a general notice that can be enclosed when such materials are sent as a result of a court order or subpoena where the expert cannot request a Protective Order so that raw data is protected.

FORM 77
Cover Letter—Raw Data
Not Released

Form 77 is the kind of letter that can be sent with the psychological report even though the subpoena requests copies of the raw data. This particular letter focuses on rules of the Florida Board of Psychology although the expert will probably find that the psychology board in his or her state has very similar rules. This letter allows the psychologists to send the final report without forwarding the raw data.

FORM 78
Request for Records by
Nonpsychologists (Forensic)—Ethical
Guidelines

Form 78 is an enclosure that can be sent to lawyers requesting records, to explain why psychologists are prohibited from sending raw data to anyone other than a qualified individual.

FORM 79
Attorney's Presence during Psychological Examination

The forensic psychologist sooner or later will find that there is an opposing counsel who wishes to be present when his or her client is undergoing psychological evaluation. This of course is unacceptable in terms of the standardization of most test instruments. In addition, Form 79 provides the psychologist with a statement that can be included in a letter to help the opposing counsel understand that this issue has been addressed in the past.

FORM 80
Videotaping during Testing

Sometimes the attorney will request that the testing procedures be videotaped and that a court stenographer be present to make an exact record of the proceedings. Form 80 presents a standard letter that can be sent to the attorney indicating the psychologist's position in respect to this request.

FORM 81
Memorandum of Understanding

Sooner or later the forensic psychologist will be asked to provide patient care for a client of an attorney. This can be a preliminary to involving the psychologist as a treating doctor and then later on trying to maneuver the psychologist into becoming an expert witness.

The standards for proper performances of forensic psychologists indicate that one should have a clear role in any case, and not develop dual responsibilities. Although frequently treating doctors perform as experts, the roles are distinct. Being a treating doctor detracts from the objectivity that one ought to have as an expert.

When the forensic psychologist believes that a lawyer is attempting to create this kind of a situation, Form 81 provides a memorandum whereby the psychologist role as a treating doctor is made clear.

FORM 82
Case Status Enquiry

At any time dùring a consultation, the forensic psychologist may find that activity ceases. Depositions are not scheduled, the court date never seems to arrive, and the psychologist is in a state of limbo as far as the records and back-up materials are concerned. Also, at the end of the case, after the testimony, the expert is again in possession of large numbers of documents.

Form 82 is useful in contacting the attorney to determine whether the case material should be retained, forwarded to the attorney, or destroyed. This is a useful form for cleaning out the files. Form 82a presents this form as it would be completed and sent to the retaining attorney.

FORM 83
End of Contact

Form 83 is useful as a closing note. After all back-up material is disposed of, per Form 82, this end of contact form is the last word in the file. Form 83a illustrates how this form may be used.

Form 76   Notice That Test Materials Require Qualified Reviewer

IMPORTANT NOTICE

THE ENCLOSED MATERIAL IS OF A HIGHLY
TECHNICAL/SCIENTIFIC PSYCHOLOGICAL NATURE.
UNDERSTANDING AND INTERPRETATION REQUIRES
AN APPROPRIATE BACKGROUND.

INTERPRETATION BY UNQUALIFIED INDIVIDUALS
MAY BE SUBJECT TO BIAS, DISTORTION OR
MISINTERPRETATION.

Form 77   Cover Letter—Raw Data Not Released

Dear Counselor:

Pursuant to your subpoena received [Date] I am enclosing a copy of my psychological report on [Name]. Also enclosed you will find my review of records provided to me.

The rules and guidelines of the [State Name] Board of Psychology require that I forward raw psychological data only to psychologists qualified to interpret such raw data. If you would designate a licensed psychologist to receive this raw data I shall forward it posthaste.

Very truly yours,

Addendum:

Florida Board of Psychology

Rule 59AA-18.004(3)—A psychologist who uses test instruments may not release raw test data, such as test protocols, test questions, or written answer sheets, to any person other than another licensed psychologist or in response to a judge's order. When raw test data is released pursuant to this paragraph, the psychologist shall certify to the service user or the service user's designee that all raw test data from those test instruments have been provided.

Rule 59AA-19.005(7)—A psychologist may not release raw test data, such as test protocols, test questions, or answer sheets, except to another psychologist or in response to a judge's order. When raw test data is released pursuant to this paragraph, the psychologist shall certify to the service user or the service user's designee that all raw test data from those test instruments have been provided.

Form 78   Request for Records by Nonpsychologists (Forensic)—Ethical Guidelines

Psychologists who deal in forensic evaluations are frequently asked for raw data and copies of test protocols. The pertinent guidelines and codes which address this issue are as follows:

A. General Guidelines for Providers of Psychological Services (APA, 1987):
   1. **Principle 2.2.3**   Providers of psychological services are familiar with and abide by the *American Psychological Association's Ethical Principles of Psychologists, Specialty Guidelines for the Delivery of Services, Standards for Educational and Psychological Testing, Ethical Principles in the Conduct of Research with Human Participants* and *Guidelines for Computer-Based Tests and Interpretations.*
   2. **Principle 2.3.7**   Raw psychological data (e.g., test protocols, therapy or interview notes, or questionnaire returns) in which users identified are ordinarily released only with the written consent of the user or of the user's legal representative, and are released only to a person recognized by the psychologist as competent to interpret the data.

B. Ethical Principles of Psychologists and Codes of Conduct (1992):
   1. **Principle C**   Psychologists uphold professional standards of conduct, clarify their professional roles and obligations, accept appropriate responsibilities for their behavior, and adapt their methods to the needs of different populations.
   2. **Principle 1.6   Misuse of psychologists work.**
      (a) Psychologists do not participate in activities in which it appears likely that their skill or data will be misused by others unless corrective mechanisms are available.
   3. **Principle 1.24   Records and data.** Psychologists create, maintain, disseminate, store, retain and dispose of records and data relating to their research, practice and other work in accordance with law and a manner that permits compliance with the requirements of the Ethics Code.
   4. **Principle 2.02 (b)**   Psychologists refrain from misuse of assessment techniques, interventions, results and interpretations and take reasonable steps to prevent others from misusing the information these techniques provide. This includes refraining from releasing raw test results or raw data to persons other than to patients or clients as appropriate, who are not qualified to use such information.
   5. **Principle 2.06   Unqualified Persons.** Psychologists do not promote the use of psychological assessment techniques by unqualified persons.
   6. **Principle 2.10   Maintaining Test Security.** Psychologists make reasonable efforts to maintain the integrity and security of tests and other assessment techniques consistent with law, contractual obligations and in a manner that permits compliance with the requirements of the Ethics Code.
   7. **Principle 7.06   Compliance with Laws and Rules.** In performing forensic roles, psychologists are reasonably familiar with the rules governing their roles. Psychologists are aware of the occasionally competing demands placed upon them by these principles and the requirements of the court system and attempt to resolve these conflicts by making known their commitment to this Ethics Code and taking steps to resolve the conflict in a reasonable manner.

C. Amendments and Rule Repeals Effective April 26th, 1993—Board of Psychological Examiners (Florida Statute 490, and Rule Chapter 21U):
   1. **21U-18.003   Disciplinary Guidelines (T).** Delegating professional responsibility to a person or persons whom the licensee knows or has to reason to know are not qualified by training or experience to perform such responsibilities. The usual recommended penalty shall be a six month suspension immediately followed by a six month probation with such terms and conditions as set by the Board.

D. Standards for Education and Psychological Testing (APA, 1985):
   1. **Standard 6.6**   Responsibility for test use should be assumed by or delegated only to those individuals who have the training and experience necessary to handle this responsibility in a professional and technically adequate manner. Any special qualifications for test administration or interpretation noted in the manual should be met (APA).

Summary:
These citations state, in essence, that raw test data, test profiles, and test protocols be provided only to those who have the training, background, and qualifications to understand and properly utilize such basic information. In a practical manner, this would mean a licensed clinical psychologist. Certainly a report of assessment or evaluation as well as other kinds of records such as therapy notes can be provided directly to the client.

Form 79 Attorney's Presence during Psychological Examination

On occasion, the expert will be challenged by an adversary attorney concerning the examination of his or her client *in camera*. The attorney may insist that he or she has the right to be present during the examination.

There is case law indicating that the courts are aware that an attorney's presence during a psychological examination will contribute very little and could seriously disrupt the purpose and the effectiveness of the examination. This is cited in *Estelle v. Smith,* 602 F 2d at 708. Also *C. F. Thornton v. Corcoran,* 132 U.S. App. D.C. 232, 242, 407 F 2d 695, 705, 711 (1969).

The above cases can be cited when challenged by an attorney concerning this matter.

Form 80   Videotaping during Testing

Re:

Counselors:

Pursuant to your question to me on [Date] as to why psychological tests cannot be properly administered while the process is videotaped, I would respond as follows:

1. Performing psychological tests and standardized examinations in the presence of a videographer or a court reporter is a violation of the Standards of Professional Practice of the American Psychological Association and consequently a violation of the administrative rules of most State Departments of Professional Regulation.

2. The presence of either person or videocamera in the test room would have significant effect on the validity and reliability of standardized psychological tests, since the normative data was developed in the absence of such distractions.

3. The presence of a person other than the examiner, or the presence of an intrusive device would have a high probability of distorting the test taker's responses.

Sincerely yours,

Anastasia, A. (1982). *Psychological testing.* (5th ed.). New York: Macmillan.

American Psychological Association. (1985). *Standards for educational and psychological testing.* Washington, DC: APA.

American Psychological Association. (1992). Ethical principles of psychologists and code of conduct. *American Psychologist, 47,* 1597–1611.

APA Committee on Ethical Guidelines for Forensic Psychologists. (1991). Specialty guidelines for forensic psychologists. *Law and Human Behavior, 15,* 654–665.

Form 81   Memorandum of Understanding

This Memorandum of Understanding is formulated on this date between _____[Examiner]_____ and _____[Examinee]_____. Specifically, _____[Examiner]_____ has agreed to undertake the following clinical work with the above-named patient with the following understanding:

1.   _____[Examiner]_____ will be a treating doctor.

2.   _____[Examiner]_____ will not serve as an expert witness in any future legal matters associated with the clinical work noted above.

3.   If called as a witness, _____[Examiner]_____ will respond as a treating doctor and not as an expert witness.

_____
[Examinee]

_____
[Witness]

_____
[Date]

Form 81a   Memorandum of Understanding

This Memorandum of Understanding is formulated on this date between _Theodore H. Blau, Ph.D._ and _Jason Updike, Esquire_ . Specifically, _Dr. Blau_ has agreed to undertake the following clinical work with the above-named patient with the following understanding:

1. _Dr. Blau_ will be a treating doctor.

2. _Dr. Blau_ will not serve as an expert witness in any future legal matters associated with the clinical work noted above.

3. If called as a witness, _Dr. Blau_ will respond as a treating doctor and not as an expert witness.

_____
Theodore H. Blau, Ph.D.

_____
W. Riggs
[Witness]

_____
_3-12-98_
[Date]

Form 82   Case Status Enquiry

In re:

We were retained as experts/consultants in the case cited above. Please inform us of the current status by checking the appropriate boxes and returning this form in the enclosed envelope.

☐ Case still active

☐ Keep all records sent to you

☐ Case settled or closed

☐ Destroy records sent to you

☐ Return all materials to referring attorney

Comments:

_____

_____

_____

_____

_____

_____

By: _____

Thank you,

Form 82a   Case Status Enquiry

James Furst, Esquire   April 23, 1998
21 Gomer St.
Galvers, Illiana 21743
In re: Jones v. AMD Corp.

We were retained as experts/consultants in the case cited above. Please inform us of the current status by checking the appropriate boxes and returning this form in the enclosed envelope.

☐ Case still active   ☐ Keep all records sent to you

☐ Case settled or closed   ☐ Destroy records sent to you

☐ Return all materials to referring
   attorney

Comments:

_____

_____

_____

_____

_____

_____

_____

                                    By: _____

                        Thank you,

                        Jason B. Roberts, Ph.D.

Form 83   End of Contact

Name: _____   Date of Closing: _____

Service: _____

_____

_____

Additional Comments:

Form 83a   End of Contact

Name: _Jones v. AMD Corp._   **Date of Closing:** _5-14-98_

Service: _1. Neuropsychological evaluation for Mr. Furst (Plaintiff's attorney)_

       2. Deposition for opposing counsel

       3. Testimony before Judge Gray, 2-11-98

Additional Comments:

1. Jury awarded $750,000 to Mr. Furst's client.

Practice Planners™ offer mental health professionals a full array of practice management tools. These easy-to-use resources include *Treatment Planners*, which cover all the necessary elements for developing formal treatment plans, including detailed problem definitions, long-term goals, short-term objectives, therapeutic interventions, and DSM-IV diagnoses; *Homework Planners* featuring behaviorally-based, ready-to-use assignments which are designed for use between sessions; and *Documentation Sourcebooks* that provide sample forms, handouts, and records for every aspect of treatment.

Practice *Planners*™

For more information on the titles listed below, fill out and return this form to: John Wiley & Sons, Attn: M.Fellin, 605 Third Avenue, New York, NY 10158.

Name _____

Address _____

Address _____

City/State/Zip _____

Telephone _____ Email _____

Please send me more information on:

- ❑ The Complete Psychotherapy Treatment Planner / 176pp / 0-471-11738-2 / $39.95
- ❑ The Child and Adolescent Psychotherapy Treatment Planner / 240pp / 0-471-15647-7 / $39.95
- ❑ The Chemical Dependence Treatment Planner / 208pp / 0-471-23795-7 / $39.95
- ❑ The Continuum of Care Treatment Planner / 208pp / 0-471-19568-5 / $39.95
- ❑ The Couples Therapy Treatment Planner / 208pp / 0-471-24711-1 / $39.95
- ❑ The Employee Assistance (EAP) Treatment Planner / 176pp / 0-471-24709-X / $39.95
- ❑ The Pastoral Counseling Treatment Planner / 208pp / 0-471-25416-9 / $39.95
- ❑ The Older Adult Psychotherapy Treatment Planner / 176pp / 0-471-29574-4 / $39.95
- ❑ The Behavioral Medicine Treatment Planner / 176pp / 0-471-31923-6 / $39.95
- ❑ The Complete Adult Psychotherapy Treatment Planner, Second Edition / 224pp / 0-471-31922-4 / $39.95
- ❑ TheraScribe® 3.0 for Windows®: The Computerized Assistant to Psychotherapy Treatment Planning Software / 0-471-18415-2 / $450.00 (For network pricing, call 1-800-0655x4708)
- ❑ TheraBiller™ w/TheraScheduler: The Computerized Mental Health Office Manager Software / 0-471-17102-2 / $599.00 (For network pricing, call 1-800-0655x4708)
- ❑ Brief Therapy Homework Planner / 256pp / 0-471-24611-5 / $49.95
- ❑ Brief Couples Therapy Homework Planner / 256pp / 0-471-29511-6 / $49.95
- ❑ The Child & Adolescent Homework Planner / 256pp / 0-471-32366-7 / $49.95
- ❑ The Psychotherapy Documentation Primer / 224pp / 0-471-28990-6 / $39.95
- ❑ The Clinical Documentation Sourcebook / 256pp / 0-471-17934-5 / $49.95
- ❑ The Chemical Dependence Documentation Sourcebook / 304pp / 0-471-31285-1 / $49.95
- ❑ The Couples & Family Clinical Documentation Sourcebook / 240pp / 0-471-25234-4 / $49.95
- ❑ The Child Clinical Documentation Sourcebook / 256pp / 0-471-29111-0 / $49.95

Order the above products through your local bookseller, or by calling 1-800-225-5945, from 8:30 a.m. to 5:30 p.m., est. You can also order via our web site: www.wiley.com/practiceplanners

WILEY
Publishers Since 1807

Disk Information

Disk Table of Contents

Disk Information

Introduction

The forms on the enclosed disk are saved in Microsoft Word for Windows version 6.0. In order to use the forms, you will need to have word processing software capable of reading Microsoft Word for Windows version 6.0 files.

System Requirements

- IBM PC or compatible computer

- 3.5" floppy disk drive

- Windows 3.1 or later

- Microsoft Word for Windows version 6.0 or later or other word processing software capable of reading Microsoft Word for Windows 6.0 files.

NOTE: Many popular word processing programs are capable of reading Microsoft Word for Windows 6.0 files. However, users should be aware that a slight amount of formatting might be lost when using a program other than Microsoft Word.

How to Install the Files onto Your Computer

If you would like to copy the files from the floppy disk to your hard drive, run the installation program by following the instructions below.

1. Insert the enclosed disk into the floppy disk drive of your computer.

2. Windows 3.1: From the Program Manager, choose **File, Run.**

   Windows 95 or later: From the Start Menu, choose **Run.**

3. Type **A:\SETUP** and press **OK.**

4. The opening screen of the installation program will appear. Press **OK** to continue.

5. The default destination directory is C:\BLAU. If you wish to change the default destination, you may do so now.

6. Press **OK** to continue. The installation program will copy all files to your hard drive in the C:\BLAU or user-designated directory.

Using the Files

LOADING FILES

To use the word processing files, launch your word processing program. Select **File, Open** from the pull-down menu. Select the appropriate drive and directory. If you installed the files to the default directory, the files will be located in the C:\BLAU directory. A list of files should appear. If you do not see a list of files in the directory, you need to select **WORD DOCUMENT (*.DOC)** under **Files of Type.** Double click on the file you want to open. Edit the file according to your needs.

PRINTING FILES

If you want to print the files, select **File, Print** from the pull-down menu.

SAVING FILES

When you have finished editing a file, you should save it under a new file name by selecting **File, Save As** from the pull-down menu.

User Assistance

If you need basic assistance with installation or if you have a damaged disk, please contact Wiley Technical Support at:

Phone: (212) 850–6753

Fax: (212) 850–6800 (Attention: Wiley Technical Support)

Email: techhelp@wiley.com

To place additional orders or to request information about other Wiley products, please call (800) 225-5945.